A TIME TO WEEP AND A TIME TO LAUGH

The Reverend Canon Robert Donkin

L.R. Price Publications Ltd

A Time To Weep And A Time To Laugh

Published by
L.R. Price Publications Ltd, 2019
27 Old Gloucester Street,
London, WC1N 3AX
www.lrpricepublications.com

ISBN:- 9781916467934

Acknowledgments

The Author would like to thank my wife for her encouragement, advice and suggestions whilst writing this book and for reading through a life story she knows very well!

The Author would also like to say thanks to The Venerable Richard A Seabrook SSC for his incentive in creating this book.

Then there are the endless people, some of whom are mentioned by name, who have been a source of inspiration and given me the motivation to write this book.

Also my past mentors, most of whom are deceased and mentioned who have led me along this path of life.

The Publisher would like to thank the following people: Len West, Susan Woodard, Matt Vidler and Russell Spencer for their hard work and support in making this book a reality.

A TIME TO WEEP AND A TIME TO LAUGH

The Reverend Canon Robert Donkin

A TIME TO WEEP AND A TIME TO LAUGH

Aberaman, 1997

'For everything there is a season, and a time for every matter under heaven: a time to be born, and a time to die.'
Ecclesiastes 3:1

You know those precious moments, after starting work at six a.m., with just breaks for meal-times and coffee? Well, they are cherished, but often rare. Especially if a funeral prevents a normal meal-time!

One such opportunity usually presented itself before Evening Prayer. With the daytime chores seen to (although, like a housewife, a priest's work is never done), a short break before going to church always allowed me to assess the evening service/meeting/interview, or whatever was in the diary. I was just settling down to a nice cuppa, in front of the computer in my study, an hour before joining my colleague for Evening Prayer in church, when the phone rang. Should I answer it, I pondered, or let the infuriating thing go into the answer mode? Better answer it - might be somebody in need.

"Hello, is that Reverend Donkin?"

O Lord, I thought, *here we go...*

Reverend, indeed? I've never felt very reverend! *That's better than Vicar or Rector,* I thought, *which usually means they're State Christians.* If they ask for Father Robert, then they are either faithful parishioners, or most likely priest-friendly folk!

I answered: "Yes, it is. Who's speaking, please?"

"This is the Bereavement Officer from Eastbourne District Hospital. I'm afraid I have some bad news for you: I have to inform you that your stepmother has died."

It took a moment for this news to sink in, and some tea went down the wrong way, which must have sounded at the other end of the line as if I were traumatized.

"I'm sorry - you must be quite upset. But, we had to ring and inform you, as you are the next of kin."

Next of kin, I thought, *what's she talking about?* After some deathly silence, I said: "Well, actually I didn't know I had a stepmother... Well, yes I did... but... well... I've never met her."

"Really? How extraordinary! We had to break into her flat... you know, she was a bit of a recluse. She died here in the hospital and no-one came to visit her."

Was she suggesting that I had neglected this woman, who was part of a life from which I had been excluded?

"The police found your letter to your late father in her bureau - the one you wrote in 1971. That's how we pieced things together and traced you. They were very helpful at Saint Michael and All Angels' Theological College, in Llandaff, and were able to give us your current address easily. We also have a letter here that he wrote to you; obviously it wasn't posted, and it is half-torn up, but I can let you have it in due course."

I reeled at this news. Will I ever be able to live my life without the ghost of my father emerging or, in this case, his floozy?

"But, this is mad: I've got the letter he wrote to me here..!"

Eastbourne, 1971

'Give justice to the weak and the fatherless; maintain the right of the afflicted and the destitute.'
Psalms 82:3

"Oh, my God, Elsie - look at this. I knew this would happen one day - I knew it. She obviously hasn't informed the boy about how things really were. Read this!"

St. Michael and All Angels' Theological College,
Llandaff,
CARDIFF.
7.10.71

Dear Father,

I expect reading this that you must be really shocked - to think that I'm nearly 21 years old and we've never seen each other and now, after all this time, I'm writing to you. I don't really know why I am, but there we are - life is very strange, isn't it? I suppose what has brought this on is the fact that since the divorce came through, I've found your address – I didn't know it before.

It would be really great to hear from you. I would love to know all about you, what you are doing, etc. I have often wondered if you ever think about me or Mum at all. Do you? I quite often think about you – they say curiosity killed the cat. However, I think there's more than curiosity concerned. Mum rarely talks about you, and I know very little about you or your marriage to her. Only once have I seen a photo of you and that was in your wedding album. I expect you've changed a bit since then! As for me, you can see from my address that I'm studying theology; I hope to be ordained priest in about 3 or 4 years' time. I have only just arrived at this college; last year I was at St. John's College in Ystrad Meurig – this is a small village in mid-Wales. There I did a pre-theological course, because I was so young.

You may be interested to know that both my grandparents are dead. My grandmother died 6 years ago and my grandfather last

December. My aunt is also dead - Mary, Dick's wife. She had a tumour on the brain and had an operation last year to remove it. However, the tumour grew back again and she had another operation last Friday, but died on Sunday. I had to go home for the funeral yesterday.

I have a girlfriend and we are getting engaged at Christmas.

Well, enough about me. I would really love to hear about you. By the way, if ever you happen to be anywhere near Cardiff, you may like to visit me in my college.

Your son
Robert.

"You must write back straight away, George, and put him off, gently but firmly. I bet he's after money. Oh, my God, this is awful! We need to get married as quickly as possible, otherwise he will have a claim on everything. If you go before me then I could end up penniless - getting married will confirm that I am the next of kin."

"Oh, don't be silly, Elsie - it won't come to that. Look at the profession he's chosen: he's not going to see you go without. In any case, there's part of me in him, you know."

"Yes, George - that's what I'm worried about!"

"Okay, okay, I'll go and write this minute."

"And I'll ring the registrar!"

"Well, if we wait a few years he could do the ceremony!"

That's when Elsie clocked him on the head with the telephone directory, before George scuttled off to the bureau, to write to his long-lost son. It wasn't easy, and there were a few drafts; however, eventually something was put to paper:

22 Rangemoore Drive
Eastbourne
3.11.71

Dear Robert,

I was very surprised to receive your recent letter and to learn of your hopes and aspirations. Nevertheless, I find this a most difficult letter to answer. Let me say at the outset that I have no desire to hurt your feelings, but I feel that no useful purpose would be served by our meeting, as the passage of time has so altered the scene, and the circumstances are so changed, that the gulf *could never be bridged. In any case, I am now divorced finally from your mother and I have remarried. My marriage to your mother was a complete failure from the start and should never have happened, and it was the best thing when she walked out, twenty years ago. As I have now remarried and I am very happy, it would be grossly unfair to my new wife to be confronted with a situation such as this.*

I do wish you every success in your chosen career and hope you have chosen the right girl, and will be happy.

Yours sincerely
Your father.

She didn't walk out on you - you threw her out, bastard!!

What sort of person can sire a child and disown it? The consequences of such actions have far-reaching effects, I'll have you know, Georgie-Porgie. However, I do forgive you and I pray for the repose of your soul. And if things were different, and we could meet tomorrow, I'd love it!

Aberaman, 1997

'Do not judge, and you will not be judged; do not condemn, and you will not be condemned. Forgive and you will be forgiven…'
Luke 6:37

"Sorry, what was your name again?"

"Mary Evans*, the Bereavement Officer at Eastbourne District Hospital."

"Well, I can't understand how you have his letter to me - I've got it *here*! It came in response to that letter you found from me."

"How odd. Would you mind making a copy of the letter you have and sending it to me? Perhaps I can throw some light on all this?"

"No problem - I'll do it right away and you should have it in the morning."

"Okay, I'll be in touch as soon as I have some news. 'Bye for now."

I fished out the letter and read it again - it was curt and formal, and I wondered why I hadn't binned it years ago.

My wife Val arrived home from school later that day, and I said: "Guess what."

A non-plussed look on her face made me say, amusingly: "I'm bereaved: my stepmother has died!"

It took a while for it all to make sense, as I explained the day's events over our usual rendezvous cuppa in the kitchen, after our respective days' assault-course, which some people call work.

The next morning the phone rang - it was Mary Evans the Bereavement Officer.

"Robert, I'm afraid the letter you received wasn't from your father - it was from Elsie."

"Elsie?"

"Yes, I've checked the handwriting: it's hers. She must have looked at the letter your father wrote, decided it was not *off-putting* enough and written her own version. She must have started to rip his letter up, but then thought better and tucked it away in the bureau, where we found it, next to your letter to him.

"I'm really sorry about this, Robert - it must be a bit disconcerting. I will send you a photocopy of the letter and you can have the actual one when the solicitor hands you some bits and pieces - he will be in touch with you. He's very nice; his name is Mister Keith Norton of Smart and Spicer. I'll post this copy off to you today, so you should have it in the morning. Is that alright...? Robert?"

"Yes... sorry, I was miles away... Thank you for your help."

The next day, the post brought Elsie's copy of my father's letter to me. Although it was still a 'put-off', it was a little nicer, and it did make me shed a tear at the time, I have to say.

22 Green Meadow
Rangemoore Drive
Eastbourne
1 November '71

My dear Robert,

It was nice to receive your recent letter and to learn of your hopes and aspirations. Nevertheless, I find that it is a most difficult letter to answer. Let me say at the outset that I do not in any way desire to hurt your feelings – you are, of course, my flesh and blood, but I feel that no useful purpose would be served by our meeting. The passage of time has altered the scene and circumstances so changed that the gulf could never be bridged.

In any case, the divorcing by myself from your mother, finally and irrevocably, after a separation of twenty years, is now complete. I have, as you know, remarried, and it would be grossly unfair to my wife to be confronted with a situation fraught with sorrow and distress.

I do hope that, even at a time when you are

on the threshold of both manhood and a lifetime career, you will understand how difficult it is for me to write this letter. I do wish you every success in your chosen career and will ever have a thought of you in my mind.

Yours affect
Father

Could he not spell 'affectionate'? Or was he 'affected' by my letter so much that he and Elsie were married on 30th November - just twenty-three days after my letter to him!

She was Miss Elsie Eton, but had changed her name to Donkin by deed-poll years ago, so they could live together without scandal, in those dinosaur days. Now, they were legally married and they needn't worry about this irritating brat who had turned up.

The phone rings again...

"Hello, Father Robert speaking..."

"Hello, my name is Kelvin Stephen Horley-Loxley - I'm a solicitor from Eastbourne. I understand Missus Mary Evans - the Bereavement Officer from Eastbourne District Hospital - has rung you, regarding your late stepmother."

"Yes, that's right; it's all a little intriguing and a bit of a surprise."

"I must say that I fully understand how you must be feeling - my wife is going through a similar situation as yours at the moment, with her estranged father - so I will do everything I can to help you through this."

"Thank you."

"At the outset, can I just say that there is no inheritance, I'm afraid."

"Well, that never entered my head - I hadn't thought about that at all. This whole thing has been a bit bewildering."

"I do understand. I have a copy of the will, some old passports, some photographs, slides, their wedding certificate, his birth certificate and a few other documents that may be of interest to you. Perhaps I can send them on to you."

"Well, actually, my wife and I were thinking that we would come to Elsie's funeral. It might bring some closure to all this and I could see where my father is buried, where they lived, etcetera."

"Excellent. I will be at the funeral with Mary and we can meet you there; I will have all these effects for you."

"Okay, that's fine."

**Name changed to protect identity.*

Eastbourne, 1971

'Whoever divorces his wife and marries another commits adultery against her…'
Mark 10:11

"There we are: married at last! Aren't you going to carry me over the threshold?"

"Not after living together since nineteen-sixty-eight, no! Tell you what, though: I'll carry you into our room, at the hotel in Capri, when we get there for our honeymoon!"

"Don't bother: you might pull your back out and ruin the holiday. Have you made all the bookings – flights, et-cetera?"

"Yes, all booked for June. It'll be really nice out there at that time - not too hot."

"Oh, I can't wait. It will soften the blow from all this."

"So, marrying me was a blow?"

"You know what I mean!"

"Well, we haven't heard from him again, so the letter must have worked. I do feel guilty, though: he is my flesh and blood, after all. Perhaps we should have had him up here and explained things, face-to-face."

"Oh, I don't think so - training to be a vicar, he would be mortified at our lifestyle: living in sin all these years! I wonder what made him choose that as a career."

"Oh, the family were all big in the Church, from the old man right down to the kids."

When I learned the truth later in life, and realized that my parents were finally divorced, I used to tease my mother that she was free to find another man! I felt I should say this, in case she worried that I would disapprove and be a difficult stepson, in the company of a new "dad".

Her response was this: "When I made those vows in Saint David's Church, it was for life, as the prayer book teaches!"

I couldn't help feeling awed at her determination. Later, when the Mothers' Union changed its ruling and allowed divorcees to be members, one of her friends rang her up gleefully, to share the news:

"Oh, Hilda - great news: the Mothers' Union is now allowing divorcees in. You can join!" said May.

"I don't think I will May, thanks all the same."

"Why not, love?"

"They didn't want me when I needed help and support as a deserted mother, so I'm not sure I want anything from them now!"

Eastbourne, 1997

'Just as a father has compassion for his children, so the Lord will have compassion for those who fear him.'
Psalms 103:13

Well, Val and I went to the funeral. It was epic.

"I'm not sure this is such a good idea, after all. Do you suppose there'll be long-lost relatives, who might be a bit antagonistic?" I said.

"Of course not - they won't even know who you are," said Val.

I needn't have worried, as it was just the solicitor, the Bereavement Officer, Val, myself and the organist present.

The hospital chaplain took the funeral and began his eulogy with the words: "None of us knew Elsie." At this point, the organist's eyes became like chapel hat-pegs and nearly popped out. The chaplain did a great job, knowing the circumstances - he gave her a dignified send-off and said all the right things; we couldn't help feeling sad, especially at the graveside.

However, at least I saw where my father was buried, although the stone had been removed.

Years later, my daughter, Rebecca, ended up working for the Glyndebourne Opera Company, and one of her colleagues lived in nearby Eastbourne. When Rebecca moved back to Wales to work once again for the Welsh National Opera Company, Val went up to help bring some of her belongings home. They went to say goodbye to her colleague in Eastbourne and Val wanted Rebecca to see where her grandfather was buried. So, they went and took a photo of it, now with Elsie's inscription added.

If George and Elsie hadn't been so panicky they could have left their flat to me, as compensation for never having met, known or loved a father. Ironically, it would have been a great help for Rebecca, living and working in that area, and a wonderful retirement home for me and Val. But, there you are: from the moment I was conceived he didn't want to know; my consolation is that worthy charities benefitted, instead.

As a young boy, I always thought he was dead, but when I found out the truth I was devastated, and it was even more weird growing up without him, then. In today's society, this story is one amongst a million other similar stories of broken families, but in 1950 it was a bit of a scandal.

REV. CANON ROBERT DONKIN

Neath, 1949

'It is not good that the man should be alone; I will make him a helper as his partner.'
Genesis 2:18

"'Ilda, you're too fussy - you'll be left on the shelf! How many men have you turned down now? You're nearly forty, girl!"

"Well, the one I really want I can't have - you know that."

"It isn't good to marry cousins: there can be health problems, especially when children come along. So, don't be so fussy."

Fussy? That was rich, coming from my grandmother, really, who had my mother baptized as Iris Matilda Richards. She then decided to call her 'Ilda, for short, which wouldn't confuse anyone, because her first initial is *I*, in any case. Later, she decided to add an *H*, in case any of her English friends thought all Welsh people dropped them. On top of this, her "pet" name was Tilly! How fussy is all that?!

However, this inherited fussiness was the problem really, as Hilda Richards went about her life of work and leisure armed with many different boyfriends, but couldn't choose; I have a photograph of her surrounded by quite a number. The occasion was a night out at the local dance-hall, and the man who got nearest to her heart was her cousin. The Table of Kindred and Affinity, in the *Book of Common Prayer*, allows it, and they were "head over heels", but it was frowned upon within the family.

Well, I would still have been fatherless, because he died suddenly.

Desperation must have set in, because Aunt Emmie and Uncle Albert, in London, were consulted and found themselves in the role of matchmakers. Surely the dizzy heights of London must procure a suitable, dashing male, to tickle the fancy of this fussy dame! Well, it turned out that they lived in Edgware and the one they had in mind was a forty-one-year-old, quite smart "chappie", who worked at that time for Rover – although, by trade he was a carpenter and joiner - and had a house of his own. This was surely good enough for forty-year-old fusspot Tilly: London, Rover, house of her own… even if it was Edgware! So, a holiday was arranged with Aunt Emmie and Uncle Albert, and a "chance" meeting fixed, to bump into George. Sadly, it worked, because she brought him home to Wales.

My middle cousin's comment, in a giggling, girlie moment, was a recitation of "Georgie-Porgie, pudding and pie, kissed the girls and made them cry". Well, he certainly made Hilda Matilda cry, that's for sure.

London, 1949

'He gives the barren woman a home, and makes her the joyous mother of children. Praise the Lord.'
Psalms 113:9

"Oh, Aunt Em, he's really nice - I like him a lot. He's calling again tomorrow, to take me to the theatre."

"That's great love - I'm so glad. I know they say that matchmakers are a nuisance, but if it pays off, all well and good! He's got a house of his own, a good steady job and a car; you can't go wrong, love - can't go wrong."

"He's promised to come down to Wales in the spring, to meet Mum and Pop. I hope he's not put off."

"Well, take it as it comes; what will be, will be. Your Uncle Albert, though, is already planning his speech!"

"I think he could be the one... Yes, I think so."

"I expect he'll ask you to meet his family and all. I think they live in Newcastle-upon-Tyne - that where he's from originally, you know: a Geordie."

"He's mentioned his parents, Edith and William Donkin. I'll have to put my best bib and tucker on for that."

"You don't need to worry, love: you're a bobby dazzler!"

After much courting, with Albert and Emmie as chaperones, a

love-struck Hilda returned to Wales, planning an Easter visit from George. She, in turn, visited his parents.

It seemed that all was well. The wedding of the year was arranged in St. David's, Neath.

My grandfather was a local businessman, prominent in the Church and sitting on many secular committees in Neath. A pillar of the Church and a respected man in the town, even though he'd "had to" marry my gran! My cousins and I found that out when Gran and Grandpa celebrated their golden wedding anniversary – the dates, you know, didn't match with Hilda's birthday and the affair was quietened down; not a big social event.

My mother's wedding was, though: the wedding of the year!

Hilda was a cub-leader, known as "Bagheera" - later in life, when I was mad at her, I would be heard to call her "Bagilda". She had a "guard of honour" from her cub-scouts, my cousins were bridesmaids and page-boy, and an old friend - someone who later taught me in school - was matron of honour. The reception was in the Castle Hotel - the place to be at that time - and photographs show a worrying groom, already looking a little worse for drink. My grandparents were beaming; at last, the fusspot was off their hands.

Off to Jersey for a honeymoon, but Hilda was left with only the moon to gaze upon, in her bridal moment of glory - the honey was gone: he had slipped off to bed, a little worse for drink. Like all "sensible" girls, she chose to take no notice and carried on, triumphant. The marriage must have eventually been consummated, because shortly afterwards I was to be found lying in my mother's womb.

"Ecstatic" is the word my uncle used of her, when she found out she was pregnant. After all, what forty-year-old, who desperately wanted children, wouldn't have been over the moon, in case she were too late? It was not the case for Georgie-Porgie, though: his pudding was certainly messed up by the very idea:

"I thought you were too old to have children; I wouldn't have married you if I'd known. Well, you can rip up some of my mother's old bed sheets for nappies - I'm not spending a penny on it."

"How can you say such awful things? This is your child - your flesh and blood."

"I don't want to hear any more about it."

"Most men would be over the moon to hear such news and would only be concerned for my health. After all, forty isn't the best age to have a child!"

Being a sensible girl, she carried on regardless but, no doubt, very afraid.

I often think I could have been an abused child, running wild on the streets of London; getting up to all kinds of weird and wonderful things, by the time I was a teenager in the swinging sixties. It was not to be, though: Auntie Mary and Uncle Dick came to the rescue - the ever-gallant, protective brother of Tilly. It was the summer of 1950; where else would a brother and sister-in-law go for a holiday, but to London, to visit Hilda in her new home and share the delight of her announcement of a forthcoming birth.

Although Edgware is in Barnet, which I believe is Greater London, north, this incident could have taken place in the East End, as a pre-run episode of the modern-day *Eastenders*. With the all too evident destruction of my mother's morale, in her delicate condition, Uncle Dick took it upon himself to smash into Georgie-Porgie, not only with his tongue, but with his fists.

"You twat (one of my uncle's favourite expressions)! You twat! You're going to do the right thing by my sister, or else..."

"Or else what? What are you going to do about it?"

"This!" With that, came a punch in the face which sent Georgie-Porgie scuttling along the hallway.

My mother always said that she and Auntie Mary were terrified, huddled together on the landing. Actually, it would never surprise me if it was Auntie Mary who stuck one on him, and Uncle Dick, such a gentleman, was protecting Hilda in some corner of the proceedings.

They stormed off in the car for a run, to calm down, debating whether to ever return. After many tears and much deliberation, it was deemed the proper thing to do to return to her rightful home and not induce accusations of desertion. In fact, Uncle Dick rang my grandfather from a telephone kiosk.

My grandfather said: "Ring me back in half an hour; I'll try and get hold of our solicitor." No mobile phones in those days. So, in half and hour my grandfather had indeed spoken to the family solicitor, who said that the correct thing to do was return to the house.

The sight that greeted them, when they pulled up outside the house, was Hilda's roughly packed bags on the drive. Although it wasn't funny, Auntie Mary told me privately, once, that it was quite amusing to see half a bra sticking out of one of the cases; it sort of represented the half-baked marriage that now was.

All this was happening while I was yet lying in my mother's womb - no wonder I was deemed to be a "nervous child", by my teachers and mentors.

So, it was back to 1950s Wales, at a time in our history and culture when the finger of suspicion pointed at you if you were a rejected female, even if the innocent party - especially one who had taken so long to choose, like fusspot Tilly! Casting all humour aside for a moment, it was a very difficult time in her life - one where she was nearly suicidal, but for the wisdom of her dearest friend Nancy, who pointed to the rather large bulge that was evidence of her plight, and said: "Now, pull yourself together and think of that child."

No wonder I was classed in school as "highly strung". As a child, I heard this said about me so often that I had a vision of hanging from the top of the Big Wheel at Neath fair.

Neath, 1949

'Therefore a man shall leave his father and mother and the two shall become one flesh.'
Genesis 2:24

"You've got to wear a wedding ring, girl," said my grandfather.

"Why, Pop?"

"Well, for a start, if you don't then everyone is going to think that you are a single mother. Also, you can't even entertain the idea of changing your surname back to Richards, for the same reason."

"Oh, I'd never thought of that." Silence... "But, I threw my wedding ring at him."

"Noticeable that he took it back!"

"He's welcome to it - I couldn't possibly wear it now."

"Not to worry - we'll go to town tomorrow and get you a new one."

"Oh, Pop, I'm so sorry about all this."

"It's none of your fault. You just concentrate on that child you are carrying; there's got to be a purpose in all this."

I always wondered if he kept the ring. Maybe he gave it to Elsie. If he had, then it might have been in the box of "bits and pieces" the solicitor gave me, at Elsie's funeral. It would have been an unusual keepsake.

The actual "wedding ring" that my grandfather bought for

her was a modest affair. In the passage of time it became too tight and had to be removed; instead of having it made bigger she wore my grandmother's keeper ring. This has now come down to me and I wear it with pride.

Neath, 1950

'And call no-one your father on Earth, for you have one Father – the one in heaven.'
Matthew 23:9

Apparently, Uncle Dick used to visit my mother in hospital, when she was due, and bring flowers and all the right things - pretending to be the "dad", so as not to embarrass Hilda, in a ward surrounded by expectant mothers and doting dads-to-be.

Perhaps that was why I called him "Dad" once, when I was a small boy. This brought on a serious family discussion:

"You've got to tell the boy - he can't go on thinking that I'm his father."

"Oh, I don't know what to say to him... how to word it," said Hilda.

She didn't get around to it until I was about nine. Even then, it came after a childlike question:

"Why haven't I got a father?"

"Well, he didn't want us," was all she could say. "But, you need never worry that you haven't got a father, as you've got one in Heaven that will never let you down." That was probably the start of my very deep, spiritual relationship with God.

The answer kept me quiet for a while, but "curiosity killed the cat", remember - I was out to find Porgie and would go to any lengths. The biggest find was their wedding album, hidden away in the closet, under the stairs - at last, I had a picture of the man who had haunted my dreams for so long.

Would I stick pins in it? No, I somehow cherished it, because it was proof that I was like other boys: I *did* have a father, and my mother was not the Blessed Virgin Hilda! However, in school, whenever I had to fill in forms, I always left his name blank, even though I knew it was George.

One teacher said: "Donkin, you've not put your father's name down."

I said: "I haven't got a father, Sir."

To which he replied: "Of course you've got a bloody father boy - you wouldn't be here if you didn't!"

At this point, the class erupted into laughter. *Nervous child,* did somebody say?

Even the name "Donkin" was an embarrassment, because my classmates quickly cottoned on, from this incident, that I was *different*: a "wimp", quiet and... yes, nervous. So, they used to call me "little donkey"; the song *Little Donkey*, by Nina and Frederick (never forgiven them), was popular at the time, and here was shy Donkin coming down the school corridor, to a rendering of that wretched song. When I got home and burst into tears, my mother's religious attempt at putting things right was to say:

"Well, a donkey is a very blessed and beautiful animal - Jesus rode on the back of one."

Try telling that to the bullies in school, I thought. That was when I really learnt how naïve my mother could be, as much as I loved her.

I noticed, in later life, that my children were never taunted in this way about their surname, which proves it really was all Nina and Frederick's fault.

Neath, 1952

'The Lord sustains them on their sickbed; in their illness you heal all their infirmities.'
Psalms 41:3

At aged fourteen months I became very ill and nearly died, through "pink disease".

Nobody's ever heard of it, which is why you are suddenly looked upon as if you've landed from another planet. It was mercury poisoning - this was found in teething powders, which were administered innocently by all who wanted to keep their children calm, during this growth period. No doubt, today the firm responsible for making the medicine would have to pay out enormous amounts of compensation, but then, well...

"You've just got to get on with it I'm afraid, my dear," said the doctor.

"Oh, the poor little chap - he looks like a tomato," said Auntie Mary.

"Hush, girl – don't let Hilda hear you say that," said Gran.

"We need salt," said Hilda; "loads of salt."

The "pink disease" was so called because one's cheeks flared up rather reddish, like a woman at that time in life... you know. Salt was diminished from the blood and had to be administered at every stage of digestion: baby-food, baby-milk, soft drinks, desserts all had to have salt added. I could have been an advocate of *Blood Pressure Rules, OK!*, especially with the flaming-red cheeks. I was lucky not to have died as a baby, and I now know why I have so many and various irritating allergies - it all came from this serious poisoning as a baby. Poor Hilda: after the shame of her marriage break-up and returning to gossip and speculation, she then had to push this flaming-red-cheeked creature around in a pram, all over Neath. "Poor Hilda and Robert" was to be heard, far and wide.

While my childhood was bewildering on the one hand, it was cosseted on the other. I had three "mothers", all living under one roof: there was my own, Hilda, my grandmother, Maggie and Auntie Mary, all fussing and spoiling. Also, I had three cousins, in place of brothers and sisters. What more could I want...?

A father?! It was at this time that I used to dream about the "perfect dad": he would have to be young, rich, famous, handsome and intelligent. Georgie-Porgie certainly didn't match up to this ideal, so I felt I needed to find one. Everywhere and anywhere I fantasized about this superhero, who would come and tuck me up in bed, take me for sports and games, and just be the most perfect father that ever was.

I thought I'd found him once: my friends and I went off to the Neath fair on a Saturday morning - after all, it was just around the corner from where we lived. The fair wasn't open yet, but that was what appealed to us kids the most: we wanted to be part of it. The stallholders were setting up, the engineers were checking the rides; we could peek into the sideshows and see the performers getting ready, until they shooed us off: the

Fat Man at the fair - I must tell you about him later - the Ugliest Man on Earth, Gypsy Rosa Lee, the Fire-Eater, the Naked Lady, the boxing booth, the World's Smallest Woman... they were all there and many more.

But, it was the boxing booth which attracted my attention - the proprietor was setting up and practicing with the punch-bag. My friends were more interested in the Fat Man, but not the Naked Lady - we found out later that that was a swizz: she wore a body-suit; it dawned on us when we noticed that she had no nipples! I was mesmerized with the boxing man. Not that I like boxing - never have, never will - but there was something about him that fitted the bill. By the time my mother came looking for me, a little anxious that I was late for lunch, I was inside his caravan, and he was telling me all about his travels, up and down the country and even in Europe. I knew, there and then, that I wanted to run away with the fair; each year that passed was a lost opportunity to do this.

Hilda took me home, berating me for talking to strange men, and that I *actually went inside* his caravan was just the most appalling thing I could have done! My grandmother nearly had apoplexy, my grandfather was all set to go and give the man a "good talking to" and Auntie Mary and Uncle Dick were convinced my father had something to do with it, and was in on the plot.

The Neath fair had a tremendous influence on me. In later life I was to take parish bus-trips there, as it was so huge, and practically the whole town was lined with stalls, rather like Petticoat Lane. I was always so proud of it, because I had been brought up with it.

Our family links with it went back further than my fascination: before I was born, my grandfather was the landlord of the Tiger Inn, on Angel Street, Neath - it stood where a supermarket now does business. There were many tales of pub-life, and Hilda used to talk of the days when the Neath fair came.

One old boy, who was a sailor and had travelled the world, always wanted to hear my mother play the piano. She hated it, but was always coaxed into performing in the bar. One particular favourite, called *Buds and Blossoms*, became a family favourite, and we all, as children, learned how to play it, much to my mother's annoyance. I used to tease her mercilessly, later in life, even though all this was way before I was born; I used to say: "You could have become as famous as 'Tilly the Ivory Tinkler'!"

She could even have had a job in the fair - I could have grown up a "fair boy", as they were known. We got friendly with a few of the "fair boys" – they would come to school temporarily, when the fair was in town, by arrangement between parents and the headmaster. We were in awe of them: they were special; heroes - what a privilege to have one in our class!

Neath Council shifted the fair from the specially-built fairground - surrounded by roads called Fairfield Road, Fairfield View and Fairfield Lane - because they wanted to build an ugly, modern civic-centre on the site. They put the Great Fair of 1280 - always opened on the Feast of the Nativity of the Blessed Virgin Mary - on a piece of land between the canal and the River Neath! I was disgusted: how dare they?! All my lovely fair-friends would have to walk through mud to get to their caravans.

I can remember being on the Big Wheel, and frightened for the first time in my life on that ride - not because of the dizzy heights, but because on the way down I wondered if we would all end up in the canal! Apparently, there were heated discussions about it - my grandfather was on the Chamber of Trade, as a businessman, and they all wanted the best for the fair people, because they had been coming for centuries and brought good trade to the town, and visitors from far and wide. They moved the fair again, years later, to a strip of land between the railway station and another section of the river.

Neath, 1956

'For surely I know the plans I have for you, says the Lord, plans for your welfare and not for harm, to give you a future with hope.'
Jeremiah 29:11

My mother always picked me up from school: Alderman Davies' Church in Wales Primary School.

One day, there was no sign of my mother, but Auntie Mary was there to pick me up. That was good: I loved her and she was great fun. I did question why, but was told that Mum had to do some business in town and would be home soon.

The business was in the Neath Magistrate's Court, I found out afterwards: there, George Donkin had been summoned for a legal separation. Hilda wouldn't give him a divorce in 1950s Britain - being a "good church girl", she claimed she had made the vows for "better or for worse" and "for life".

It was "for worse", but by today's standards I would have been among thousands, and it would have been a common, everyday affair. It certainly wouldn't have had the constraints of a legal separation - it would simply have been *divorce*. Only film stars divorced in those days, apparently.

She named me after her favourite film star, Robert Donat, because she couldn't find a name to go well with Donkin! That, however, was the only link with Hollywood. If they'd had trouble finding a first name, they quickly gave up with a middle name! For one horrible moment it may have been "Isaac", after my grandfather, but my gran said:

"No, absolutely not!"

When asked why, she said: "His initials will be R-I-D, and we don't want to get rid of him, especially as his father did."

Years later, I was to berate my mother and remind her of all the saints' names that there were in Christendom, her being a good church girl, and all that! Born on St. Martin's day, I should have been named after him.

The nearest and dearest call me "Rob"; Uncle Dick and a few other members of the family used to make me cringe, when they called me "Bobby". No-one has ever dared to call me "Robbie", "Bert", "Bertie", or any other variation of this name.

Anyway, the court case, so I'm told, was over pretty quickly. All the family were there, except us kids and Auntie Mary, of course. George apparently was stony-faced and hardly looked at anyone throughout the proceeding, except for glaring at the magistrate. There was no fight over custody, as he never wanted to see me, ever; the only wrangling was over money - he had to give the statutory amount, as maintenance, to my mother.

The magistrate said, in all innocence: "Now, Mister Donkin, how much are you going to give towards the maintenance of your child?" Sadly, the magistrate must have thought that any normal, warm-blooded father would have wanted to be generous and know that his child was provided for, even if the marriage was "half a bra".

George, however, said: "How much do I have to give?"

"Twelve and six."

"That will do."

After a stunned silence in the courtroom, the magistrate turned to my mother and said: "Missus Donkin, if I were you, I would go home and rejoice that this person does not want to have anything to do with you or your child."

So, it became a joke, years later, that I was only worth 12/6d anyway - and that was "old money", remember? I've always seen the funny side of this. If I'd been naughty, I can hear my gran now: "Leave the boy alone - he's only worth twelve and six, anyway." It did actually increase every year, with the rate of inflation, and in the end it reached thirty shillings!

"Thirty pieces of silver," my uncle remarked, one day.

Neath, 1957

'He saved us and called us with a holy calling, not according to our works, but according to his own purpose and grace.'
Timothy 1:9

"The Body of our Lord, Jesus Christ, given for thee..."

Gran said: "What the hell is he doing? There's pieces of paper all over the front room floor and he's saying prayers, or something."

Hilda: "I'll go and have a look."

Gran: "Don't spy - you might embarrass him!"

"...the body of our Lord, Jesus Christ, given for thee..."

Another piece of paper fell to the floor. Didn't they know that I was practicing for the day I would be doling out pieces of bread, and not pieces of paper?

Hilda and Gran were shocked. They had realized I was copying the rector, from Sunday morning, but I was only eight, had only just joined the choir at St. David's, and had a bullseye view of what went on around that altar.

"You've gone white, Ma," said Hilda.

"I've just remembered the rector's words to you, when you were carrying him. Do you think this is an omen?"

The front room at 6 Angel Street - formerly the Tiger Inn – was, to us children, the *magic* room. It's where the floor to ceiling Christmas tree was housed in the festive season; it's where our toys lived - the most amazing playroom - and in the days when it was the Tiger Inn, it was the bar. It's where Tilly would have tinkled the ivories.

Outside and across the passage was the door to the cellar. This was where they used to shelter from the bombs during the war, and it's where all the booze used to be kept, when it was the Tiger. It was a scary place. Once, when they were hiding there during an air raid in the war, Gran apparently commented on Auntie Mary's pregnancy that sitting there on a deckchair, waiting for the Germans to go, she was due to drop! Not a bomb, but a baby. Gran said: "Please, please don't let the baby be born tomorrow."

"Why?" said Hilda.

"It's Hitler's birthday!"

Fortunately, the baby came that night. After the bombs, she went to hospital, making it by the skin of her teeth.

What a house that was! Upstairs was a maze of rooms and little corridors, which would have been the accommodation at the Tiger. It was a huge house, of three storeys. Mum and I were on the top floor with David, Diane and Susan; Gran and Grampa, Auntie Mary and Uncle Dick were on the first-floor.

When Evan's Bevan Brewery decided to close the pub, they gave my grandfather compensation and allowed him to continue renting the pub as a home. Out of his compensation money, he bought a horse and cart and started a coal-merchant's business. There was a huge backyard where the horse and cart used to be kept. By the time I came along, it was a lorry - Uncle Dick's pride and joy.

Susan and I have fond memories of Mr. Price the milkman, coming on his horse and cart, on a Saturday morning, to collect the milk money. We were always on our very best behaviour and always came into the kitchen - where he was having a cuppa with Gran - because he always gave us a thrupenny bit each; a fortune in those days.

One very exciting event was the "Great Flood of Neath". The river and the canals overflowed and the streets were flooded; it was like Venice, only not so picturesque and much smellier. I will always remember a group of young men canoeing around the roundabout outside the Tiger. It was amazing. Auntie Emmy and Uncle Albert were staying with us, and I have a photo of Albert sweeping out water, from the passageway in the Tiger, back onto the street... or should I say the "river"? Looking back, perhaps it was his penance for finding Georgie-Porgie-Pudding-and-Pie! The cellar was full to the brim and the smell was awful; we never had the same look on the house again and it wasn't long before we all moved.

Alas, life would change forever: David would go off to do his National Service, Diane would go off to join the Wrens and with the coal-business growing and doing well, it was planned we would split up and buy new homes.

Auntie Mary and Uncle Dick went first to 111 Cimla Crescent - it was very posh. People used to call it "Kipper and Curtain Crescent" - it was alleged that people would eat nothing but kippers to be able to afford the very best curtains. Other people commented that the people there were "all furs and no knickers". None of this was true, of course: Auntie Mary certainly wore knickers! She and Uncle Dick deserved a beautiful new home: after all, poor Mary had lived with her in-laws for quite a long time.

Later, the rest of us - Gran and Grandpa, Hilda and I - would move to 89 Cimla Road. Actually, in those days it was 29 Upper Cimla Road, until someone with a brain in the council determined that it was all one road and just needed to be re-numbered.

It was the summer of 1958 and I was seven when we left the Tiger for a newly-built house. It was like a dream.

Neath, 1961

'God chose what is low and despised in the world, things that are not, to reduce to nothing things that are.'
Corinthians 1:28

"Please, Heavenly Father, don't let me have to carry the cross this morning. It's too heavy - I'm only eleven! Please, let Evan Parker be there this morning to carry it. Please... please!"

On my way to St. David's, this was often my prayer.

I just couldn't cope with the idea of me doing anything in public, leave alone carry the cross! If the rector wanted me to sing a solo I would die of shock; if he asked me to read, I'd be beside myself. It was all the fault of Georgie-Porgie, I convinced myself: it was because of him that I had such low self-esteem and shied away from everything.

I'd joined the choir as an eight-year-old and became awed at the rector, Father J.F. Williams. He had a wonderful teaching and preaching gift as a priest. He was extremely musical and taught us boys how to sing, organizing choirboy courses via the R.S.C.M. Mostly, they were held in Lampeter, but one or two were held in Darley Dale, near Derby. I attended five altogether, and they really boosted my confidence; to this day I will say that they prepared me for singing Mass, and offices in church.

We had such a lark on these courses. Can you imagine about thirty or more boys, all living together in a college, the only supervision being housemasters, who couldn't wait to get to the bar? They waited until we were all settled in bed, in the dormitory - they actually walked around each bed to make sure we were settled! I used to imagine that my particular housemaster would have made a good dad. Once they had gone, we would put the lights back on and have a whale of a time.

The whole week was geared towards a Choral Evensong, cathedral-style! It meant a lot of hard work, to achieve a high standard, but it was worth it in the end. The culmination was Choral Evensong, in the college chapel, on the Sunday evening at the end of the week, to which parents were invited. After the service, they took us home, rejoicing at our achievements.

The night before Choral Evensong - the Saturday night - there was always a concert, with contributions by willing students. At one of these courses, J.F. (as we called the rector) mentioned to the organizers of this ad-hoc concert that I could play the piano.

"No, I can't do that - I'm not that good!" said I.

"Nonsense - you'll be fine," said my housemaster.

Nothing I could do would persuade him otherwise and, to this day, if he knew how much I agonized over playing the piece I had chosen, he would, I'm sure, be very apologetic. I had to spend nearly all of Saturday practicing one of Chopin's waltzes. I was so nervous on the night that I couldn't tell you now whether I was any good or not; people clapped anyway. I featured last and had to sit through the whole thing, waiting my turn; I couldn't wait to get to the party, afterwards!

At home, in Neath, we performed some solos and anthems

on the ensuing Sundays - things we had learnt on the course. J.F. presented us and told the congregation how proud he was of our achievements.

J.F. wasn't afraid to say it like it was! There was one "old girl" in the sopranos, called Cassie Lawrence - her voice was amazing, and we laughed behind her back, calling her "the curdled larynx", because we felt that her larynx must be just that. J.F. insisted that she sat at the back, out of sight, and preferably out of earshot.

Lent and Holy Week was always a very important time in the life of the parish. Each year, J.F. would get someone to preach at a weekday evening Mass in St. David's, every Wednesday in Lent, starting, of course, with Ash Wednesday; the same person would preach at every service in Holy Week, and finally on Easter Day. This person could be a monk, a nun, a priest he knew from England, or a lecturer from a theological college, and they were always inspirational. It was one particular Holy Week which inspired me to attend a weekday Mass on my way to school, from then on; at first, I went just once a week, but when I knew that one of my mother's dearest friends attended every day, I decided to do the same.

She was, of blessed memory, Auntie Hettie, whose son is now a priest. I was privileged to be part of such a wonderful parish, with such a superb priest as rector. His daughter sings with Val in a chamber-choir now, and we often reminisce. He often called to the house to speak with my grandfather, who was a churchwarden, and I was so shy I would pretend to be occupied upstairs, until I was called down to say hello - it was rather like meeting the headmaster at school.

How times have changed in Caerphilly? I would walk down the high street and men used to say: "Alright, butt..." while women would say: "Alright, babe..."

Neath, 1962

'If the Lord does not build the house, in vain do its builders labour.' Psalms 127:1

One day, the rector announced some startling news: they were going to build a new church "up the Cimla". That's where I lived! What was going on?

Well, my grandfather and my mother were in on it: the rector had asked my grandfather to be the people's churchwarden.

This was unique to the Church in Wales, as the constitution declared that the priest should appoint his own rector/vicar's warden and the people elect a people's warden - that's how it should be, always. However, we now had two wardens chosen by the priest! So, another gentleman from the congregation - Bill Powell - was chosen to be his rector's Warden, for this yet unbuilt church; my mother was to be the Sunday school superintendent.

The whole project was regarded by the people at St. David's as a mission to the "ungodly" people of Cimla. Years later, when it was announced in St. David's that Robert Donkin was to begin training for the priesthood, you could see it on their faces and almost hear it under their breath: "Can anything good come from the Cimla?"

It was enormous fun. The first building was an old Nissen

hut, donated by Llandarcy Oil Works. It was swiftly converted inside to a dual-purpose building: church-hall by week, church on Sunday, with a sliding partition. We had a choir, youth club, Sunday school *a la "Bag-hilda"*, and loads of new friends. There was only one snag: I wasn't allowed to go.

The rector said: "Donkin, you must continue in the choir at Saint David's."

"But, Father, all my family will be at Saints Peter and Paul's."

"No, I won't have it - we need you in the choir."

"But, can't I join the choir in Cimla church?"

The answer was a resounding: "NO!" You couldn't answer the rector back, not like today, when people call me "butt" and "mate", and tell me to "f- off"!

So, there it was: separated from my family at worship. I can't remember how long it took me to rebel but, with a gang of youth club members and the curate, we marched on said rector and told him what for. I distinctly remember hiding behind the curate at this point.

Unbelievably, Father J.F. agreed and for a moment I was overjoyed, until he said: "But, you've still got to get to the choir in Saint David's by eleven a.m., Donkin!"

Oh, hell! How would that work out?

Well, whoever took the service in Ss. Peter and Paul would give me a lift down to St. David's. That was fine, except for Sundays, when the rector was taking the service. I'd have to sit in the car with Almost-God Almighty and talk to him, all the way to town; I was a shy, nervous child, remember. After the service in St. David's, I would have to walk all the way back up to the

Cimla.

Well, thank God, we had a new curate come soon. Full of himself, he was, and he seemed to have a way with the rector. He had come from the cathedral, and that somehow made him awed. He made the rector see sense, telling him that he wanted me to be a server, chorister, reader, cross-bearer and anything else he could think of, to save my soul and make his plea sound good. It worked: I was allowed in to Ss. Peter and Paul's Church, fully, with my whole family.

The said curate was a great inspiration to me, and without him and the rector, I wouldn't be where I am today, as I have said. When I told him I thought I wanted to be a priest, but didn't know whether I was up to it, he said: "What the hell makes you think I am?" From that moment on, he included me in everything and took me to all special services in the cathedral, driving through all the country lanes in the Vale of Glamorgan, in those pre-motorway days - a short-cut route I was to use later, making my way to St. Mike's.

Neath, 1962

'A people whom you do not know shall eat up the produce of your ground and all your labours, and you will never be anything but oppressed and crushed continually. You shall be driven mad by the sight of what you see.'
Deuteronomy 28:33

"Oh, for God's sake, don't let the boy see these - put them away in the sideboard, before he finds them," said my gran.

Hilda said: "He's not interested in newspapers at his age."

I was coming down the stairs of 89 Cimla Road, when I heard these comments. What on Earth were they talking about, I wondered - as an eleven-year-old, I was intrigued.

It was a Sunday and I knew they would all have a nap after lunch… that would be my time! Indeed, after they'd all had a sherry and were full on their lunch, it was dishes, then crash out. I waited patiently and crept into the dining-room, when they were all snoring; opening the sideboard door, I found the Sunday papers - my grandfather liked to have various political opinions, so purchased three or four each day.

It was about the trial of Adolf Eichman, who had been captured in Argentina and brought back to Israel - it was sensational international news. I opened the first one and read the headlines:

"Nazis murdered 6,000,000 Jews in 'Death Camps'!"

What is a "death camp", I thought. ...*Death camp...!*

There were vivid pictures of ovens, in which human-beings had been burned after being gassed; there were stories of severe beatings, hunger and starvation; days-long train journeys from various parts of Europe, where people were stuffed into cattle-trucks, many of which died on the journey; no sanitation; no water; no food... often in extreme heat. Upon arrival at these "death camps" some people were sent immediately to the gas chambers. Others were unlucky enough to be used as slave labour.

"Doctor" Mengele did various experiments on people for the good of the Aryan race, and he was exceptionally interested in twins. Some people were thrown into ice-cold water for a while, then into boiling water, so he could assess the effect.

These people were treated as animals. The S.S. were trained – or, should I say "brainwashed" - into believing that these people were sub-human, and therefore deserved brutal treatment and death. When the allies were approaching, they were so desperate to kill as many Jews as possible that they were throwing live children into the ovens - they couldn't be bothered to waste time gassing them first.

It wasn't just Jews - 30,000 priests were exterminated, for speaking out against the Nazis, as well as thousands and thousands of Polish people, because they were deemed sub-human, alongside the supreme perfection of the Aryans. Homosexuals were rounded up and received gross treatment from the guards, just because they had been born that way.

I cried. I couldn't believe it. How could human-beings do

this to others? At the age of eleven I declared that I absolutely hated Germans - what a stupid race of arrogant bastards they were! At all anniversaries of the Holocaust, there was always a plethora of films on television about the subject, and this didn't help.

It took a long time for me to realize that this manic behaviour could happen in any country in the world, where there is unintelligent hatred towards minority groups. As I write, there are rather a lot of such uneducated bigots in *not-so-Great* Britain, who would see all kinds of minority groups done away with.

Now, I am learning German, and what a great language! I can see now how difficult it must be for German folk to come to terms with the past.

Two heroes stand out for me, from this devastating time in our history:

Firstly, Father Maximilian Kolbe, a Polish priest who died at Auschwitz. After somebody had tried to escape, the guards had rounded up about ten or more prisoners to execute them, as an example to everyone who had ideas of trying to escape. One very young man cried that he had a wife and children - Father Max stepped forward and told the guards to let the man go and take him instead. It took a long time for him and the others to die in the underground death-bunker, from starvation and dehydration - no food or water was given to them. Before they became emaciated, the guards could hear hymns being sung and prayers being offered to God.

Years and years later, Pope John Paul II beatified Father Max.

On that day, the young man - now grown up and a survivor - together with his children and grandchildren, were in St. Peter's Square for the occasion.

The other hero is Karl Leisner, who was a deacon. He was arrested for saying something against Hitler, imprisoned at Dachau and confined to the priests' block, in harsh conditions. He suffered from T.B., which became worse, and his hopes of being ordained priest seemed hopeless. Then, Bishop Gabriel Piguet, of Clermont-Ferrand, arrived in Dachau as a fellow prisoner, in 1944. Clandestinely, through the help of a young woman - Josefa Imma Mack, who was later to become a nun – he brought the necessary letters of approval, along with holy oil, stole and ritual books, and the ordination of Karl Leisner took place in block 26, in secrecy. Hundreds of clergy prisoners supported the young deacon, who wore an alb over his striped prison clothes. A Jew played his violin to distract the guards, and Protestant ministers all helped in this ceremony. Father Karl celebrated his first - and last - Mass, on 26th December: St. Stephen's day - the first martyr; how significant is that?

When the camp was liberated, he was very near to death. Father Karl Leisner was beatified by Pope John Paul II in 1966.

Austria, 1938

'Arise, Lord, let men not prevail! Let the nations be judged before you.'
Psalms 9:20

"Mama, there's our house!"

"Hush, girl - it's not ours anymore."

"But, I left my doll in the bedroom - I want to get it."

The Anschluss had taken place on 12th March that year, and Heidi and her family had been evicted from their home, which had been commandeered by the invading Germans. A large, imposing house looked important enough for them to administer their filthy, murderous, Nazi ideology.

The car stopped at a junction and before they could realize it, Heidi had slipped out of the car, and was crossing the road toward their house.

Heidi's mother screamed out of the window: "Heidi, come back, please - it's not safe!"

"I'm going to get my doll."

They had no alternative but to find somewhere to park and make their way to their former home.

"What do you suppose she'll say to them?"

"I've no idea. You know how headstrong she is."

"Well, we'll have to play it by ear and be full of apologies."

"Yes. If they realize it's our home they might think we are

trying to find important documents they think we may have hidden - you know how fanatical they are?"

"Just act coolly."

"Hello, little girl. Who are you?" said the Nazi officer.

"I'm Heidi and this is my house. I've come to get my doll. Who are you?"

"I'm Hans. Shall we go and look for your doll?"

"My bedroom is on the second floor. I just hope that Gretchen, our maid, hasn't hidden it away somewhere."

"Well, let's go and have a look, Heidi."

"Yes, here it is! Gretchen must have forgotten to pack it."

"Well, sit here until your parents come - I'm sure they won't be long. They must be worried about you."

"They fuss too much."

"What's your doll's name, Heidi?"

"It's 'Gerta'."

"That's a pretty name for a doll."

"Oh, here they are."

"Heidi, what have you done? I'm so sorry, Officer - she slipped out of the car when we stopped at the junction, and we had to find somewhere to park."

Heidi and Hans were sitting on the bottom step of the staircase, talking about her doll.

"Don't worry, Mutter - she has found her doll and we are all very happy. What a delightful little girl you have."

"Oh, thank you, Sir. We'll be on our way now and won't disturb you any longer. Come along, Heidi - say 'thank you'."

"She said this was your house."

"Yes, before the Anschluss."

"Don't worry - it will be returned to you when the Third Reich has accomplished her mission in this world."

"See," said Heidi: "I told you it was our house."

Heidi's mother paled, caught hold of her daughter's hand and made hastily for the door.

Heidi, one of my parishioners, told me this story and it fascinated me. In church discussion groups, inevitably the subject of evil in the world would crop up, and it wouldn't be long before the Nazis and their brutality would come up in discussion; Heidi would never say anything. I questioned her once and she told me how much they had suffered. Although she was Austrian, and although the Germans marched into Austria and declared Anschluss, the majority of normal Austrians hated it.

Neath, 1962

'And you will hear of wars and rumours of wars. See that you are not alarmed, for this must take place, but the end is not yet. For nation will rise against nation, and kingdom against kingdom, and there will be famines and earthquakes in various places.'
Matthew 24:6

"Well, if Khrushchev presses that red button then at least we'll all go together," said my gran.

"What's she talking about, Mum?"

"Don't worry, love; Kennedy will sort it out - there won't be a nuclear war."

"What's going on?"

"There's been a build-up of aggression between America and Russia - one country threatening to drop a nuclear bomb on the other."

Goodness, I thought, *what a state on the world.*

To lighten the mood, Hilda fished out a card, from a box in the closet under the stairs, and gave it to me. "It's your ration card, from the second world war."

"But I wasn't alive during the second world war."

"No, I know love, but rationing went on for a number of years after the end of the war."

"Really? Why are you giving it to me now?"

"Well, if Khrushchev presses that red button and there's

chaos in the world, you might need it!"

We laughed and laughed but Gran frowned, saying we shouldn't joke about such serious things.

It came to nothing, thank goodness, and we all thought the world had learned a lesson...

...not so!

The Cuban missile crisis of October 1962 was a direct and dangerous confrontation between the United States and the Soviet Union, during the cold war, and was the moment when the two superpowers came closest to nuclear conflict.

Fourteen years of food rationing in Britain ended at midnight on 4th July 1954, when restrictions on the sale and purchase of meat and bacon were lifted; this happened nine years after the end of the war.

Wow! I always think that I just missed the war by the skin of my teeth. That's why I have such an interest in that period of history, with all the consequences: the Nazi invasion of Europe, the Holocaust, fascist ideology... you name it. It was never taught in school, as it had only just happened, so in a sense it wasn't really considered to be history. If it had been taught in school, then perhaps it would have helped me greatly to understand this difficult time in history.

Many years later, when I was a curate in Mountain Ash, two foreign students came to stay in the parish. One was Serge, a French student, and the other was Karin, a German student; they were on placement in Mountain Ash Comprehensive School, as part of their teacher training experience. Serge lodged next door to me, with Miss Edith Powell, and Karin lodged with Wendy and Glyn Davies, who were part of the party-going gang I found myself a part of.

Karin and I met up now and again, and I quickly realized that she wanted to consider me her boyfriend. Well, there were so many complications: different country, different culture... but, most of all, she wasn't a Christian. I could quickly see it was never going to go anywhere and my thoughts bore fruition, one Sunday lunchtime.

We'd cooked lunch together and enjoyed a typical British Sunday lunch, with all the frills, which she had grown fond of, at Wendy and Glyn's. She was impressed with my cooking skills and was eager to learn how to make a typical British Sunday roast. After the main course we had dessert: trifle; how British is that? Then, we decided to settle down and watch a film; how traditional and British is *that*? A Sunday afternoon film.

When she was in the bathroom I switched the television on and selected a film; it had already started, but only just. When she returned from the bathroom she looked at the television, gasped and then exclaimed: "Oh, typical! How bloody British: a war film! Can you people never get over it? You won the bloody war; we know - there's no need to harp on about it!"

With that, she grabbed her coat and left, slamming the door behind her, and that was the end of that.

I wondered for days and days afterwards what her father did in the war. Was there an element of guilt lurking there? Was he a guard in a concentration-camp; was he high up in the Nazi hierarchy; had he overseen the execution of Jews? I couldn't help pondering about her abrupt exit from my house - it wasn't logical.

When I told Serge all about it the next day he was very sympathetic. He said he would speak to her, but I said: "No, don't bother - it was never going to work, anyway."

Serge told me about how his family had suffered badly when the Germans had invaded France. Some of his parents' best friends were Jews, and had been rounded up like cattle and shunted off to death-camps. His grandfather had been beaten up for sympathizing with some Jews who frequented his grocery store. Toward the end of the war his grandfather was struggling to keep in business, because most of his produce had to be shipped off to Germany - little was left to sell to his fellow French customers. Poverty, hardship and struggling to survive became a way of life, until the war ended. I couldn't help admiring Serge, for the way he had befriended Karin.

She may have been an Aryan blonde bombshell, but her Teutonic nature would have been quite a challenge in the Church in Wales!

Neath, 1963

'Awake, my soul; awake lyre and harp, I will awake the dawn.'
Psalms 57:8

It was a thing called "Beatlemania", and it swept the world in a very short time. The music was awesome, and each day every newspaper featured them on the front-page, inside pages, centre-pages… the T.V. news featured them nearly every day. T.V. chat shows wanted them, America wanted them, the Queen gave them MBEs. Shops everywhere sold Beatles things: chewing-gum with snapshot cards (I have them today and can still sniff the gum); Beatles boots, elastic-sided…

"Please, Mum, please can I have elastic-sided shoes with Cuban heels?"

"Oh, love, you know what Grampa will say!"

"I know: '*common*'!"

I wanted flared trousers, knitted ties and a corduroy jacket (*common*); barbers were advertising "Beatle cuts" (*really common*). I can remember throwing out my NHS round-rimmed glasses when I was finally allowed to have something stylish, only to find that John Lennon immortalized them; I learned, then: never throw anything out! I wanted a reefer jacket, a John Lennon corduroy hat and shirts with the collars buttoned down. I became a member of the "Official Beatles Fan Club" and still have a collection of memorabilia, in a box which my kids hilariously refer to as "The Beatle Box", but is now worth a small fortune. This entitled me to *Beatles Monthly* - a magazine dedicated to all of their antics and showbiz escapades; it was Heaven. And, of course, I collected the LPs, singles and EPs; it was so exciting to go to Arthur Salter's music shop in Neath Market, to buy their latest single.

"I want *She Loves You*, please, by the Beatles, Mister Salter."

"I'm sorry, lad: we're sold out!"

"Sold out? It was only released this morning!"

"I know, I know. We'll have more in tomorrow. Apparently, it's in the top ten already! Isn't that exciting?"

Exciting? It was bloody annoying! I was a member of their fan-club, didn't they know? How dare they sell out and make me wait another day!

She Loves You entered the charts on 31st August that year and remained in the charts for thirty-one consecutive weeks, eighteen of those in the top three, including every week of September, October, November and December 1963. It reached number one on 14th September and stayed there for four weeks, dropped back to the top three, then regained the top spot for two weeks, starting on 30th November.

I used to shut myself in our lounge, in the house at Cimla, where we lived, put their music on as loud as I dared, grab a hairbrush and sing along, pretending to be John, Paul or George. Then, I'd get some of my mother's large knitting-needles and pretend to be Ringo, drumming away on the pouffe. It didn't matter that I was a shy and nervous child, and it didn't matter that I had no father: I had the Beatles - they were my heroes and gave me a purpose in life; their music will live for as long as there is life on this planet. Thank you for brightening up my bewildering teens and the rest of my life!

Whilst writing these memoirs, I have received a notification from *Spotify* that there is a "deluxe version" of *Sgt. Pepper's Lonely Hearts Club Band* being sent to me, as it is the 50th anniversary of its release. Am I that old? It only seems the other day that I scraped enough pocket-money together to buy it!

I didn't quite appreciate at the time what a huge project the album was, until a special T.V. programme I saw the other day, celebrating the anniversary, went into detail about the musical techniques applied by the boys and Sir George Martin. It changed "pop" music forever, apparently, and from that day orchestration, musical and poetic themes, and operatic styles became the norm for many musicians in the pop world. I even read the other day that, lyrically, John was very much inspired by Dylan Thomas (Dylan, of course, appears on that famous, legendary album sleeve). I always used to say to Val: "I'd love to be in the same room as John Lennon and Dylan Thomas - his poem *Quite Early One Morning* inspired the song *Good morning, good morning* on the album."

I listen to some pop music of today and I cringe, comparing it to the joyous sounds of the sixties. I feel so privileged to have been a teenager at that time - it was so exciting; and, although it all started with Chuck Berry, Elvis and Buddy Holly, it was The Beatles, with their unique sound, who made pop music what it is today. I love the Rolling Stones also, and it's a tribute to them that after fifty years they are still rolling! The Kinks also featured high on my list of idols. It says it all that their lead singers have all been knighted: Sir Paul, Sir Mick and Sir Ray. The other day, Ringo was knighted... Other legends also gave me a reason to live: Cilla Black, Sandy Shaw, Dusty Springfield, Manfred Mann, The Supremes, Martha and the Vandellas, Cher, Roy Orbison, Elvis, Cliff Richard and The Shadows, Led Zeppelin, Pink Floyd, The Seekers, The Carpenters and many, many others; their music lives on - it will never die!

People often think that the sixties was a terrible decade, of drugs, loud music and promiscuous behaviour but, looking back, for me it was a wonderful time - I am so glad I am a "sixties person"! If you take the trouble to listen to some of the lyrics from the songs of the time, you will appreciate the desire and great yearning for peace and love. John Lennon - R.I.P. - gave us *Imagine*, which has become something of an anthem - all of it was inspired by the horrors of the Vietnam War. The Byrds and their song *Turn, Turn, Turn* also springs to mind, inspired by Ecclesiastes 3:1-11; from that is the title of my book: *A time to weep and a time to laugh*.

Neath, 1966

'But Jonah set out to flee to Tarshish from the presence of the Lord.'
Jonah 1:3

I decided to run away from home.

It was no good going with the Neath fair - they wouldn't want a spotty adolescent, who spent his life in church. In any case, most of our old fair-friends would be dead by now, or retired to magnificent caravans, or not remember me anymore.

My schoolfriend, Chris Evans and I planned it all. It was the swinging sixties, and we would shoot off and form a pop-group. He had two electric guitars and said I could borrow one; neither of us could play the guitar, but why should that matter? We also had some "purple hearts", which we found out later were sherbet.

We quickly realized that we didn't have enough money to get to London and certainly not enough to set up home anywhere upon arrival, at least not for longer than a day! So, we settled for Derby! Yes, why wouldn't anyone want to enter the pop world in Derby?

So, we made arrangements for B-and-B, snuck off in the night and ended up in the swinging-less, neon-lightless, pop world-less city of Derby! Was it a city? I don't even know. Our landlady eyed us with suspicion, especially as we only had enough money for one night.

Only one night was enough, after trolling around the dead and lifeless streets of this non-swinging, non-pop world. We somehow managed to travel home without tickets, using the last of my money to ring home. Uncle Dick was there to meet us at Neath General Station, and nothing much was said. It was the return of the prodigal and I was treated as if nothing had happened, although I could clearly see that I had given my Mum hell!

It did the trick, though: I was no longer treated like a little boy, and I was respected for my choices of long hair, Beatles music, hippy clothes and wanting to hang out with my mates until reasonably late. The suffocating home life of Grandfather, Mother, the Church, school and no father was broken.

The whole episode soon became a family joke and my cousins were in awe that I'd actually had the courage to do it!

In fact, it was all Porgie's fault, really - the empty gap to this day can only be filled with a proper family set-up; mine was a good, loving family, but the lack of a father left a huge, gaping hole. Even to this day, if I'm out and about and see young families together, I immediately feel a bit envious. I see dads playing with their children on the beach, in parks, holding hands in supermarkets, etc., and I look at them and think: *Why couldn't I have had a father as lovely as that?*

Those bewildering years of my youth, particularly as a rebellious teenager, were comforted by one stupendous musical phenomenon: the Beatles!

Neath, 1967

'Ah, Lord God! Truly I do not know how to speak, for I am only a boy.'
Jeremiah 1:6

"Gosh, Gran, I'm going to be called a 'Metallurgical Inspector' and I will be on the staff of the steelworks. I'm actually going to be in charge of about thirty or so men! I'm a bit scared, being only seventeen!"

"Well, there you are, love. Isn't that a bit better than that silly *Psychedelic Boutique* you wanted to work in - could be shut down when all this beetle nonsense is over!"

"It's 'Beatles', Gran: The *Beatles* - the greatest musical entertainers in the world!"

"But, they repeat the same words, over and over again."

"So does Handel, in the *Amen Chorus*!"

"Anyway, Grampa's going to be delighted, as he pulled a few strings to get you that job. When do you start?"

"Monday."

Monday came and my boss, Mr. Bond (who didn't look anything like Sean Connery), led me down to the bay. As we walked in, one of the labourers started whistling and said to his mate: "We're going to have fun with that! Come to Daddy, sonny-boy!"

I cringed.

It turned out that Colin and Rolly were harmless and were just tickled pink that a seventeen-year-old was to be in charge of them. The language and the jokes, though, were unprintable. However, for me it was the "University of Life". I have coped with so many situations in my ministry as a priest, thanks to that experience in my young life.

Roy, one of my foremen, lived nearby, and used to pick me up if we were on the same shift. This was so helpful before I passed my driving test, especially for the morning shift, starting at 6.00a.m., and I think this put me in good stead for early morning services in church every day, as a priest. Once in Roy's car, he'd say: "Who did you shag last night?"

After Colin and Rolly's comment, Mr. Bond said: "Don't take any notice of them, lad." We continued walking down from the offices, to the bays where the steel was made.

Actually, it was fun bossing around men old enough to be my father or grandfather. They, of course, teased the living daylights out of me - when they got to know that I was a Christian and actually went to church, at the age of seventeen, that my grandfather was a churchwarden and my mother a Sunday school teacher, they were in Heaven. I can hear them now, singing a Beatles song and changing the words: "He was just seventeen..."

They had a multiplicity of jokes and I just laughed with them. However, in the staff room we had some amazing discussions about the Faith, and of those men, one in particular, called Sid, said one day: "You ought to be a vicar."

"Don't be daft, Sid - I could never do that."

"I'm telling you: yes you can and you should, I mean it."

I told our curate, Father Brian, and he agreed.

"But, I don't think I'll ever have enough confidence to preach and speak in public," I said.

"You will: the Holy Spirit will give you the confidence; how do you think I cope?

"First thing is to tell the rector."

Oh no, I thought, *that would be like telling my old headmaster. Help, I don't know whether I can go through with this!*

The day I left the steelworks to go to college, there was a row of a dozen or more chippies, who took of their caps and spoke to me: "We think what you're doing is wonderful and we wish you all the very best."

I was astonished. I thought they were going to say that they were glad I was going, because I was a cheeky little monkey!

Neath, 1968

'The Lord called me before I was born; while I was in my mother's womb, he named me.'
Isaiah 49:1

"Mum, I've got something to tell you."

"Oh yes? Nothing wrong, is there, love?"

"No. I've given things a lot of thought, I've spoken to Father Brian and the rector, and I've decided I want to become a priest."

Hilda nearly fell onto the bed, composed herself and stared at me, white as a sheet.

"I thought you'd have been pleased."

"Oh, I am, love, I am - I'm just thinking back to something that happened, when I was carrying you as a baby."

"What was that?"

"I was probably at my lowest ebb, and I went into Saint David's Church, after shopping for baby things for you, with Auntie Nancy; I settled down near the font, to have a rest and ponder over things. Not a good idea, really, as the font itself brought a new spark of panic: about names, godparents, will 'the rat' be there…? Probably not... What will people say? Auntie Nancy did her best to comfort me, and all this caught the attention of the rector, who boldly marched to the font, and brought reassurance and comfort, in his pastoral way.

"'After all,' he said, 'who knows what the child will be? If it's a boy, then perhaps the Lord might want him for a priest.'"

I should have chickened out then, really, but I couldn't, as I was trapped between the silky walls of my mother's womb.

This knowledge awed me and I felt an even deeper urge to be ordained. All those years of shyness, low self-esteem, curiosity over my father and his lifelong rejection of me, seemed not to matter so much, any more. My mother's teaching, that *I need never worry as I had a Father in heaven*, made sense. All those years of praying to him, as Father, like a frightened little boy, then later in life, in my college days in Ystrad Meurig, with his Spirit bringing me into a deep relationship with his Son, meant that I had, indeed, been called in the womb - set apart for a purpose.

Theologians would probably say this was the wrong way around: Jesus first, then *he* points you to the Father: *"No-one comes to the Father, except through me."*

Well, every other part of my life is wonky, so why should this be any different? All the many ailments I have been subjected to make me say, from time to time, that Satan has been trying to get rid of me, even before I was born! He knew what the Lord had in mind. If Hilda had jumped off the Neath bridge, as Auntie Nancy told me she was thinking of doing, then indeed I wouldn't have been born at all. Then came the pink disease, then came oesophagitis in college, then pericarditis in Bridgend, then suspected meningitis, leukemia and lupus, in Aberaman, and now coeliac disease, with many minor things in between!

REV. CANON ROBERT DONKIN

What's going to be thrown at me next?

Llandaff, 1968

'For many are called, but few are chosen.'
Matthew 22:14

"You'll have to go and see the Warden of Ordinands," said Father Brian.

"Oh gosh, I'll be a nervous wreck," I said.

I knew I'd have to go through with this, so I made the necessary appointment and Father Brian took me to Llandaff. I met Father Alan Davies, while Father Brian went off to visit old friends, from his time in the cathedral.

"Well, you're very young," said Father Alan: "you're only seventeen!"

"Yes, Father, but I really feel called to be a priest." I explained all about my churchgoing history, my witness in the steelworks, my grandfather and mother's influence, etc.

"Well, I want you to do an O-level in English Literature and come back in a year's time."

We shook hands and I went to find Father Brian, feeling a little dismayed. He gave me encouragement and said that this was typical procedure, to make sure that I was genuinely interested - some people would give up there and then. I understood, and was determined that this would never be said about me.

It was the daughter of one of my mother's close friends who

came to the rescue - Wendy coached me in my spare time, after working in English Literature.

That was the beginning of my love of Dylan Thomas and his works; his poetry and prose writings were part of the set works that year, which I had to study. It was a new experience for me, but I loved it, and to this day, my love of his works is undying. Like a lot of geniuses, his tragic life was cut short, through alcohol and living in the limelight. It always astonishes me that the Americans loved him more than we, his fellow Welshmen. I have a very precious book called *A Child's First Christmas in Wales* - it is an American publication, and was given to a parishioner in Mountain Ash by some American friends; once Marcia knew of my love of Dylan's works, she gave it to me. Priceless!

I have often been in situations in parishes - some humorous, some crazy and some downright farcical - and felt that I could be living through a scene in *Under Milk Wood*, or another of his stories.

The said O-level was achieved, and a return journey to the Warden of Ordinands planned with Father Brian.

"Good," said Father Alan. It was said with a rather surprising tone, as if he hadn't expected me to turn up again.

"Well, you'll have to go to a preliminary theological college now, to obtain a few more O-levels and get back into the swing of studying, as you've been out in the world for a while."

"Yes, alright - whatever it takes, Father. I really want this."

"It's a place in mid-Wales called St. John's College, Ystrad Meurig, near Tregaron; there will be other boys there, in a similar situation to yourself. I will make all the arrangements and you will begin at the end of next September. In the meantime, I want you to buy these books, make good use of them and join the Guild of Saint Illtyd - there you will meet up with other prospective ordinands, and have monthly meetings with me and the archbishop."

"Thank you, Father. I look forward to going to college."

When I caught up with Father Brian, I said: "Is there no end to this? He wants me to go to a pre-theological college now, for a year."

"Don't be disheartened. It's a long road to ordination, but the Lord will get you there."

"I know. If I hadn't been so eager to leave that wretched grammar school to get a job and earn money, then I might now be able to enter theological college proper."

"No, you would still have tests and hurdles to overcome before getting there."

The Guild of St. Illtyd turned out to be good fun and archbishop Glyn Simon was a lovely, humble man. He had actually confirmed me as a teenager; at the time I was rushed into Tonna Hospital with appendicitis, and had to miss the actual confirmation. When I had recovered, I had to go to Skewen church and was confirmed alongside an eighty-year-old lady. In the Guild of St. Illtyd I can recall a girl amongst us called Mary-Ann - can't remember her surname – and she hounded Archbishop Simon at these meetings, as to when he was going to ordain women! I could see how uncomfortable he was in conversation with her, and how we all were appalled at her rudeness.

"I think we're a long way off that," said the archbishop.

"Well, it's all up to you." She's probably a bishop in America now.

The day dawned to leave for Ystrad Meurig. My mother travelled with me and Uncle Dick followed, to bring her back home. She gave my new landlady - Auntie Tatty - the once over and I could see the eye contact: *watch it, lady - this is my boy!*

I asked her what she thought and the epic Hilda reply was: "Nice."

They returned to civilized South Wales and left me to the devices and desires of Auntie Tatty.

Here, a saga began!

Neath, 1968

'Thus, even my friend, in whom I trusted, who ate my bread, has turned against me.'
Psalms 41:10

My grandfather's fellow churchwarden, at Ss. Peter and Paul's Cimla, was Bill Powell.

He had served with the International League, during the Spanish civil war. In amongst all the pain and anguish of that terrible time he fell in love with a local girl: Maria. When the Falange were approaching Maria's village, some members of the League came to warn them that terror was approaching. With permission and encouragement from Maria's father and family, Bill made arrangements for her to travel to Britain, along with many others, to relative safety. World war two would soon break out, and I can only think that Maria must have felt safe in her new adopted country, even though fascism was abounding in Europe... Has anything changed? Later, when they had safely reached Britain, Bill felt it was a good move to Anglicize her name from Maria to Marie, so she could blend in and not stand out as a foreigner.

She was a delightful person and we got to know her really well. I became friends with both her sons: Robert and Andy.

One day, I had to call to their house with a message from my grandfather - some church business, which I can't recall; no wonder I can't recall it, after the story Marie told me, of her life in war-torn Spain! The civil war there seemed to have been forgotten, with all the chaos in the rest of Europe, thanks to Adolf. The day I called we had a good chat, because Bill was out; the boys were doing other things, so it was just she and I. We talked about everything under the sun: the Church, her boys, my friends and, of course, Spain. This was motivated by the fact that they were due to travel to Galicia the following week, for their annual visit to her parents, who had survived the civil war.

"The thing is, Rob, a man came running into our village from the next village down. He was wounded and gasping for breath, and shouted as loud as he could in the church square, for everyone to come out and listen to him. People were wary, thinking he was *loco*, or a Falange in disguise. He was actually a fellow brigade member, with Bill, and the message he gave made everyone listen carefully and panic…

"'They've taken all the young men who are left in the village - some as young as fourteen - lined them up against the church wall and shot them. Then, they took all the young women into the Ayuntomiento (town-hall) - some as young as twelve - and systematically raped them.'

"He gave a description of all the old women crying, and the old men wailing and despairing. The old folk didn't care anymore if they were shot - everything they lived for had been destroyed; they felt it was a punishment that they had survived and their offspring had been violated."

"Oh, my God," I said, not really understanding the agony of the reality.

"So, you can see why my father easily agreed for Bill to take me to Britain."

I felt really dismayed and had so much respect for Marie after hearing that. She was a much-loved friend to our family and we all made a fuss of her, knowing what she had been through.

She made two beautiful albs, ready for my ordination, together with cowls - they were made from pure linen bedsheets that my mother had, and they lasted years and years. I could do with them now, in sunny Spain, to allow me to breathe in all the heat.

Robert Powell took me on his motorbike once, at a high speed, down Cimla Hill to Neath town centre - I thought it was the end of my life! He had a portable cassette player glued onto the bike, and blasting from it was Led Zeppelin. Unfortunately, his younger brother Andy died of Hodgkin's disease. I was always glad this happened after his mother's death.

I was so very proud that Bill and my grandfather worked closely together, as the very first churchwardens of that brand-new church in Cimla; it was a missionary situation and created such special relationships.

Since buying our retirement property in Spain I have read many books about the civil war and I often think of Marie. Unfortunately, I have lost touch with Robert, but if he is alive, then he must still have family in Galicia.

One person told me that there are still bullet-holes from the civil war, in the walls of a cottage in the hamlet, next to our village.

REV. CANON ROBERT DONKIN

Ystrad Meurig, 1970

'First clean the inside of the cup, so that the outside also may become clean.'
Matthew 23:26

Auntie Tatty had gone off to Rhyl, for her chapel's Sunday school annual outing. I don't think there were any children left in the Sunday school, but they still went every year to Rhyl.

About a week before, I had contracted food poisoning and ended up in Aberystwyth General Hospital for tests, having to stay over. Apparently, Christopher had taken Auntie Tatty to task over her cleanliness, stating that it was her fault that I was in hospital so, when I came back to her house, I was given V.I.P. treatment for a day or two. However, when she left for the Sunday school trip, we all took it upon ourselves to spring-clean the kitchen. Mostly, it was giving surfaces a good clean and the pots and pans a good wash, to remove grease, however, Christopher decided that he was going to clean the frying-pan, in which we cooked breakfast every day - it was as black as the ace-of-spades on the inside, as it was on the outside. We told him not to bother, but he was on a mission and, after a lot of hard work, he could see his face in it.

When she came home we told her we had done some cleaning to help around the house, and she was very pleased... that is, until she saw the frying pan.

"Boys... *Bach!* What have you done to my frying pan? You've ruined it! It was a wedding present and has never been cleaned!"

"Well, no wonder Robert ended up in hospital!" piped up Christopher.

She went off in tears and we made ourselves scarce. We told the principal, to cover ourselves, and he explained that it was an old Welsh custom to just rinse the pan in soapy water and leave it to dry. We'd all been introduced to the new non-stick invention in the civilized south, so this was news to us.

Sundays in Ystrad Meurig were quite an experience.

We boys in the college formed the choir in church, served, read the lessons, etc. The service was bilingual, if only, I think, to accommodate us southerners, who couldn't speak Welsh. The organist was Miss Mair Edwards - a rather large woman - who viewed us with disdain, through her piggy eyes. We think she had a crush on Stuart and we teased him relentlessly about this.

As well as the Sunday Mass, we were expected to attend Sung Evensong, at six p.m. At the end of the psalms, of course, the *Glory be* is sung; services were, as I said, bilingual, so the *Glory be* was in Welsh. The words "As it was in the beginning is now and ever shall be world without end, amen" in Welsh, are: "Megis yr oedd yn yr dechrau, y mae'r awr hon ac y bydd yn wastad: yn oes oesoedd, amen"; we changed the opening words to "Megis y Mair and a deckchair".

We often went off in my car to visit local beauty spots, and nearby Swyddffynon had a famous feature called Devil's Bridge. Here, courtesy of *www.visitmidwales.co.uk*, is the legend of Devil's Bridge:

"One day in the olden times, old Megan of Llandunach stood by the side of the river Mynach, feeling very sorry for herself. The Mynach was in flood and roared down the wooded dingle, in five successive falls. Just below where Megan was standing there was a great cauldron, in which the water whirled, boiled and hissed, as if troubled by some evil spirit.

"Now, Megan's concern was for her one and only cow, which was on the wrong side of the ravine. How the wrong-headed animal had got there, Megan could not guess, and still less did she know how to get it back.

"'What is the matter, Megan?' said a voice, behind her.

"She turned around and saw a man, cowled like a monk. She had not heard anyone coming, but the noise of the waters boiling over and through the rocks, she reflected, might easily have drowned the sound of any footsteps.

"'I am ruined,' said Megan: 'there is my one and only cow - the sole support of my old age - on the other side of the river, and I don't know how to get her back again. Oh, dear, dear - I am ruined.'

"'Don't you worry,' said the monk: 'I'll get her back for you. It is one of my amusements to build bridges and, if you like, I'll throw a bridge across this chasm for you.'

"'Well, indeed,' said the old woman, 'nothing would please me better. But, how am I to pay you? I am sure you will want a great deal for a job like this.'

"'I am very easily satisfied,' said the monk: 'just let me have the first living creature that crosses the bridge after I have finished it, and I shall be content.'

"Megan agreed to this and the monk told her to return to her cottage and wait there, until he should call for her. Now, Megan was not half such a fool as she looked, and she had noticed, while talking to the kind and obliging stranger, there was something rather peculiar about his foot. She had a suspicion, too, that his knees were behind, instead of being in front, and while she was waiting to be summoned, she pondered so much that it made her head ache. By the time she was called for, she had hit upon a plan. She threw some crusts to her little dog to make him follow her and took a loaf of bread under her shawl to the riverside.

"'There's a bridge for you,' said the monk, pointing proudly to a fine span bestriding the yawning chasm.

"'Hmm, yes,' said Megan, looking doubtfully at it, 'yes, it is a bridge. But, is it strong?'

"'Strong?' said the builder, indignantly. 'Of course it is strong.'

"'Will it hold the weight of this loaf?' asked Megan, bringing the bread out from underneath her shawl.

"The monk laughed, scornfully; 'Hold the weight of this loaf? Throw it on and see. Ha, ha.'

"So, Megan rolled the loaf right across the bridge, and the little black cur scampered after it.

"'Yes, it will do,' said Megan. 'And, kind sir, my little dog is the first live creature to cross the bridge. You are welcome to him, and I thank you very much for all the trouble you have taken.'

"'Tut - the silly dog is no good to me!' seethed the stranger, and with that he vanished into thin air!

"From the smell of brimstone which he had left behind him, Megan knew that, as she had suspected, it was the Devil whom she had outwitted!

"And, that is how the bridge came to be known as Devil's Bridge!"

It is a feeling of great pride that a tremendously edge-of-the-seat modern-day crime drama, called *Hinterland*, is set in this very area. I can recall the place names: Swyddffynon, Pontrhydfendigaid, Tregaron, Fair Rhos and Strata Florida Abbey, to name but a few; I can remember the roads and the magnificent views as if it were yesterday that I lived there. The programme is transmitted in English, Welsh and bilingual.

Neath, 1971

'Very truly, I tell you, no-one can see the Kingdom of God without being born from above.'
John 3:3

"Hello, Mum! Great to be home!"

"Oh yes, love. Glad you're home safe."

I explained all about my last term in St. John's College, Ystrad Meurig. I talked about all my friends, and Stuart, John and Christopher, who became my very close friends. She had met them all, as I used to stop off at Mum's before giving them all a lift home – thus, I could have a break from driving. My little Morris Minor was adored, as it was a cheap form of transport away from the vast and empty - yet beautiful - space of mid-Wales.

After settling in to Ystrad Meurig, at the start of our academic year, I became a very close friend of Stuart's. He once said: "It's all very well to be calling yourselves faithful Christians, but if you're not 'Born Again', then you're not a true Christian!"

I was aghast! How dare he say such a thing? I quickly realized, of course, that I was a bit naïve - I came to understand that each of us had a different Christian experience. I also realized that it was going to be a very interesting year, for all of us.

"You have to know the Lord Jesus as your personal savior."

He lectured all of us on this and, in turn, we all challenged him that we were on the road to ordination: God had called us; there was no doubt in anybody's mind that he lived in our hearts.

"Yes, but do you really know that?" said Stuart. "Can you feel his presence? Do you know that you are saved?"

The arguments went on for the whole academic year.

Our landlady was a chapel-goer. She was only really interested in making money from the Church in Wales, by offering her home as accommodation for students, along with other villagers. The cuisine was sparse, the accommodation was basic and we were treated like schoolboys, even though we had all left school and sustained responsible jobs; she expected us to be in bed by ten p.m.! She was known in the village as Auntie Tatty - well, "tatty" was the best word to describe her food, attitude and meanness. In winter months, the fire would die down at about nine p.m., and she would wind up the grandfather clock in the hall and say goodnight to us, telling us: "Don't be long now, boys."

I was the one designated to slip down into the cellar, to collect lumps of coal to keep the fire going, because I was thin enough to get down the narrow, stone steps. This enabled us, as young men, to carry on with our theological discussions. As the night wore on, we became hungry, drinking cans of lager, hidden in our rooms.

We established a pattern, whereby we would buy tins of curry and rice, and stash them in our rooms. Then, in college, we would make sure that at the end of the lectures the kitchen window was left ajar. Late in the evening, it was always me designated to climb through the window late at night, so we could cook our curry and rice.

"Why is it always me that has to fetch the coal, always me that has to hide the food, and always me that has to climb through the window?"

"It's because you are Auntie Tatty's favourite boy!" said Stuart.

"No," I said, "*you* are, because you're the only one here who can speak Welsh."

"No, it's because she fancies you," said Christopher. A chorus of laughter ensued from Stuart, Christopher, John, Malcolm and Keith.

"Let's get on with this meal, before someone sees lights on in this kitchen," I said.

We ate heartily, had more cans of lager, then sneaked back into Auntie Tatty's house.

I shared a room with Stuart, and even then, after some serious drinking, he carried on again about being "Born Again".

On the last day of term, at the end of our academic year, as I was driving them home, Stuart made us promise that we would go to bed that night and ask the Lord Jesus to come into our hearts. After more moans and groans, we promised, just to keep the peace and shut him up.

The night I arrived home, I had a catch-up with Hilda, then went to bed, after relating many like stories with her and having a good laugh.

After reciting *Compline*, as I was dozing off, I remembered my promise to Stuart. I said: "O God, just to shut Stuart up, will you please come into my heart, even though I know you are already there? Amen."

The next morning, I jumped out of bed, opened the curtains and felt elated: absolutely full of joy, peace and love - I wanted to sing for joy; I wanted to praise God from the rooftops; I wanted to shout aloud. I opened the bedroom window - it was a glorious day, which seemed to complement my feelings, and was a sign from the Lord.

Everything fell into place: all that I had been taught, all we had studied, everything that had led me to ordination, my early relationship with God as a Father - all became consolidated. I was on fire, filled with the Holy Spirit, and I ran downstairs and told Hilda:

"Mum, remember what I told you about Stu, and my promise to him? Well, it's happened: he's come into my heart!"

"Yes, I see, love. That's nice."

That was always Hilda's response to something she didn't really like or understand. I could see that she didn't really comprehend, so I just let it go and made for the telephone, to ring Stu. He was over the moon and refrained from telling me "I told you so". I rang Christopher, who said I was a mad as Stu; I rang John and he, too, said he'd had a similar experience.

What a wonderful God we have! I knew that there was no other religion in the world that expressed the true Faith, the one true God and Jesus Christ as saviour of the world. I studied this phenomenon and was intrigued by how many people had experienced similar encounters with the Living God. Some were famous, like Helen Shapiro, a Jew, who is now a Messianic Believer. Even Muslims, risking death by changing their faith, had become believers! Why…? How…?

Through the dwelling of the Holy Spirit.

Neath, 1972

'Ask, and it will be given to you; search, and you will find; knock and the door will be opened for you.'
Matthew 7:7

A letter came for my mother one day, when I was home from St. Mike's. She read the letter and turned pale.

"What on Earth is the matter?" I said. "You're as white as a sheet."

"Nothing, love; just something from an old friend."

She wasn't careful enough hiding the letter and I spent some time, later, searching it out - I couldn't resist looking at it, because she seemed so distressed. It told her that, now the law had changed, she was automatically divorced, because after seven years it was called an "irretrievable breakdown of marriage"; of course, it had been many more years than seven.

I noted his address. I wrote it down, but I needn't have: it has stuck in my brain ever since.

"I'm going to write to the bastard! I'm going to find out the truth, once and for all. I'm going to make him tell me why he never wanted me."

Without my mother knowing, I wrote to him. It was handwritten: I couldn't afford a typewriter. In the back of my mind, I also had plans to visit 22 Rangemoore Drive.

Later, at St. Mike's, I told two very close, dear friends all about my background and they were astonished. Peter quickly devised a plan, that at the end of term I should stay with them in The Lodge and make a visit to Eastbourne, before going home to Neath.

We did, and I panicked when Peter's car pulled up outside number twenty-two! I chickened out, but Peter said he would come with me. Doris stayed safely in the car.

Alas, it was to come to nothing. A gentleman answered the door and I was dumbstruck, not only because of the situation, but also because this man didn't look anything like the photos I had of my father. Peter took control.

"Good afternoon. We're looking for a Mister and Missus George Donkin."

"Oh, sorry mate: they don't live here anymore - we bought the house off them about two years ago."

"Do you have a new address for them?"

"No, sorry, they were funny buggers - a bit shady, to say the least."

Suddenly, my tongue sprang to life: "Yes, you can say that again! Sorry to have troubled you."

"If I should find an address, would you want me to let you know?"

"Yes, please - I'll give you my address."

"Are they relatives?"

"Sort of."

Peter concluded by stating they were my father and his new wife, to a gob-smacked man, gently closing his door.

Cardiff, 1973

'And Og, the king of Bashan.'
Psalms 136: 20

So, we had decided to have a night out from the stresses and strains of studying at St. Michael's. This was tricky, as we were supposed to be in our rooms after nine p.m., studying or reading. Anyway, a gang of us had made arrangements, and off we went, into the big city.

"Where are you taking us, Nicholas? I don't trust you," I said.

"Ooh, listen to him, with his cocky Saint Michael's voice, calling me 'Nicholas' - whatever happened to 'Nick'?"

"I haven't forgiven you for singing *I Want to be Bobby's Girl*, in that pub in Canton last week - you playing the piano and everyone singing along... that was fine, until you started that song, sunshine, so watch out!"

"We're going to the 'Showbiz Club', in the centre of Cardiff."

"*Showbiz Club*? That sounds a really seedy dive, I must say."

"You'll love it, trust me."

We arrived, paid our entrance fee of fifty-pence, and we all ordered gin and tonics - they cost fifty-pence each, also. It was very dimly lit, the music was too loud, we could hardly hear each other, so we couldn't tell Nick what we thought of it. David had a plan that we would just grab Nick and usher him out onto the street, then find somewhere else to go - we just needed to find him, in the darkness and the crowd.

We sat, supping our gins, when suddenly all the lights came on and the music stopped. We were too stunned by the state of the place to notice the police: the walls were painted black, the empty crisp packets and cans on the floor made it look like a rubbish tip, the dense smoke (what was that smell?!), the drunken bodies strewn here and there, and the boys-dancing-with-boys and girls-dancing-with-girls took us by surprise, until we realized that this was a drugs raid!

Everyone was interviewed, and names and addresses taken. Did we know this was a gay club? asked the officer, when he heard our address.

"NO! Where's Nicholas - I'll kill him!" I said.

We returned to St. Michael's and somebody had locked the side door to the kitchen, which we had left open - alas, we had to walk through the car park at the back of the college, into the quad. Here, we sought out windows of boys we knew well and whose lights were still on - the only one was Nigel's, on the top floor. We had to find small stones to hit his window; this took a while, but eventually he opened his curtains and window.

"What the hell is going on?"

"Long story," said Christopher.

"Explain later," said John.

He let us in and, over coffee, we explained our dilemma.

"So, where is Nick now?" said Nigel.

"We're not sure," I said, "but when I get hold of him he's in big trouble."

The police had informed the warden of St. Michael's, and the next day we were each, in turn, asked to go to his study. We all thought it was the end of our hopes for ordination, but Canon O.G. Rees was actually quite bemused by the whole thing. He was extremely intellectual and couldn't quite bring himself to call it the "Showbiz Club", saying instead: "I understand you have visited the 'Show Business Club', in Cardiff."

"Yes, Father, but it won't happen again. I'm sorry."

"Yesss (he always emphasized the s), not quite the place for a prospective priest."

Each one of us had the same talk and we sighed with relief that it could all be put aside. Never again! One highly embarrassing thing was that one of the policemen who interviewed us was from Neath and lived in the police houses, not far from where I lived - worse than that, he recognized me!

O.G. Rees was nicknamed "Og". Whenever *"Og, the king of Bashan"* was recited in the psalms at Morning or Evening Prayer, the whole college of boys would increase volume and almost shout: "...and Og, the king of Bashan!"

Llandaff Cathedral, June 28th 1974

'Before I formed you in the womb I knew you, and before you were born I consecrated you.'
Jeremiah 5:1

We lined up in the processional way in the cathedral, all in our shining, new dog-collars!

In St. Teilo's Priory, our place of ordination retreat, we had laughed at the sight of each other dressed as clerics, waiting to be taken to the cathedral. The priory was run by the Community of the Holy Name - the sisters were a tremendous influence on me. I had to give Sister Renate a lift to a local church once, as she was giving an address; she was German and we talked about everything under the sun, there and back. We had such a lot in common, as she too had been blessed with a Born Again experience! On the morning of ordination, she clasped my hand and gave me a wonderful smile - a *knowing* look!

Sister Joy was another gem! She lived out her name and after morning prayer, in their beautiful chapel, she gathered us together and said a little prayer with us, before we made our way to the cathedral.

All ready to leave the priory, the laughter had gone - we were now as nervous as lambs!

After robing in the prebendal house, we made our way to the processional way. The dean said a vestry prayer and the organ boomed out the tune for the hymn *Disposer Supreme.* My legs nearly gave way and I wondered if I would make it up the aisle.

The service was wonderful and I felt thrilled and awed to be part of it. The choir was tremendous; the organ blasting away, the solemnity of it all and the packed cathedral brought a lump to my throat.

"Does anyone know of any just cause or impediment why these persons present may not be ordained to this holy office?" said Bishop Stephen.

Goodness me, I thought, *I'd forgotten about that part of the service!* I wondered if anyone would shout out that Donkin swore, smoked, drank and was totally unsuitable. Would the pillars holding up the majestas collapse on me?

I got away with it, anyway!

One year later, at my ordination to the priesthood, the numerous hands pressing down on my head made me realize that there was no going back!

I looked down at my family and could see they were awed; Hilda was beaming! My cousin told me afterwards that it had counteracted Mum's low self-esteem from a broken marriage and feeling of rejection, big-time.

What awed me most at the time was that statement by the rector, all those years ago - it had been fulfilled...

"Hilda, you don't know what God wants that child for; if it's a boy, he may be a priest!"

Nowadays, only a few selected people are allowed to come forward, for the laying-on of hands, at the ordination to the priesthood. Such a pity, as it was a tremendous thrill to have all your friends, mentors, etc. supporting you at that momentous event. Also, today it is the custom to have a reception somewhere, after the service, but in those days it was straight off to your parish - maybe there would be a little get-together somewhere, but nothing significant.

Actually, it was the day of the parish summer fete, in Mountain Ash, and I was taken there by Father Gwilym, as it was in the vicarage gardens. What an introduction to parish life - everyone gawking and commenting: "Oh, is that the new curate?"

Heather, his wife, said: "All the young ladies will be lining up to meet you soon!" She was sort of joking, of course… sort of!

St. Michael's, 1974

'As you have sent me into the world, so I have sent them into the world.'
John 17:18

"Well, where are you being sent?" asked John.

"Mountain Ash," I said.

"Mountain Ash?" came an astonished chorus of replies.

"That's all sheep and coal," said Nick.

We had been summoned to the common room, and each of us Llandaff boys had to go to the bishop's palace, to be told which parish we were being sent to. When one boy returned, he announced who was next to go.

Bishop Stephen told me that Gwilym Williams would be a wonderful training incumbent and that his wife, Heather, would mother me. All that turned out to be true, and I couldn't have had a better start.

In fact, I never saw any sheep and the coal industry was waning. What I did have, though, was a congregation of very intellectual and well-to-do people - that scared me to death, at twenty-three years of age. We had at least six J.P.s, three doctors, two solicitors, two head-teachers, several teachers, a plethora of businessmen and, of course, Lord Aberdare, when he was in residence. It kept me on my toes, with regard to homily preparation and the celebration of Mass.

I can remember my first homily there, very well:

"Are you alright now, my boy?" said Gwilym.

"Yes, I'm fine - you've read the homily, you've listened to me delivering it, so all should be well."

He went off to make last minute preparations, before the service was due to start; I continued robing in the sacristy.

He came charging through the sacristy door, white as a sheet. I said: "Whatever's the matter?"

"Lord Aberdare and his family have come - they came home last night and have taken up residence in Cefn Pennar House. They're all sitting in the family pew!"

"Oh, Lord," I said.

"Do you want me to preach, instead?"

Silence...

"No, I'll do it: in for a penny, in for a pound."

"Good lad."

The whole family were very complimentary afterwards, as were the congregation - I think they felt for me, having a peer of the realm just yards away.

What a happy ministry I had there. They say that you have a special place in your heart for the parish where you served your title, and that is certainly true in my case. It's where I met my beloved wife and became included in her wonderful family. It's where I learnt so much, from so many wonderful people.

Mountain Ash, 1974

'Then was our mouth filled with laughter, on our lips there were songs.'
Psalms 126:2

It was a parish dinner, to mark the start of a new stewardship campaign. The golf club in Mountain Ash was booked and about fifty or sixty people attended; it was a great venue and the meal was exceptional.

"Heather," I said, "where are the toilets?"

"Just through the hallway there and first right, my love," she said, gesturing.

Off I went and settled myself in a cubicle, wondering why there were no urinals.

Alas: female voices!

"Gladys, love, you won't believe these new tights from Marks - they're like the old silk stockings we used to have, before the war."

"Really?"

"Oh, they're great, and so reasonable."

I froze, realizing that Heather had directed me to the ladies'. More voices:

"Lovely night, girls."

"Oh yes. Wonderful meal."

"Oh yes - really great."

"I was just telling Gladys about these new tights in Marks."

"Oh, I know - I had some last week, when I went to Cardiff."

Silence...

Hair was being adjusted, lipstick being re-applied, more face powder administered...

"Well, do you think there's someone in that cubicle? We've been here a while, now - it must be empty, but it's locked. Hope there's no-one in there, unwell."

"Perhaps we should call a member of staff."

"No, I'll give the door a try, first - maybe it's just stuck."

Confident that it was securely locked, I held my breath, praying for them to go.

Alas, it swung open!

Gladys screamed and declared: "Oh my God, it's the new curate!"

I hastened to make a swift exit, without looking back. "Sorry, ladies, the vicar's wife directed me here by mistake. I'll leave you in peace."

Peace? I thought. *Just wait until I get back to our table. How embarrassing! Only been in the parish six months; this is bound to be gossiped about, from one end of the town to another!*

Indeed it was, but Gladys later said that I had "carried it off with great dignity".

Dignity?! Was there any left?

"Heather!"

"Did you find them, my love?"

"Oh yes, I found them, alright - you directed me to the

ladies'!"

Silence...

Laughter erupted and Gwylim said: "The gents' are down there, in the opposite direction."

I explained that I would now be the source of much amusement in the parish, and indeed the whole town. Heather was full of apologies and said that she would explain and make things alright.

What a nightmare!

Mountain Ash, 1974

'Feasts are made for laughter; wine gladdens life, and money meets every need.'
Ecclesiastes 10:19

A knock on the door!

"Good morning. Can I help?" I said, in my best new-curate's voice.

"Hello, my name is Cliff Scurlock and I just wanted to introduce myself to you. I believe you are the new curate at Saint Margaret's Church, is that right?"

"Yes, Mister Scurlock, I am."

"Please call me Cliff, and accept this as a housewarming present." He gave me a litre-bottle of Walker's Scotch whisky.

"Oh, thank you very much. That's so kind."

"You can thank me by letting me take you to lunch one day."

"Well, that would be lovely."

We fixed a date and it turned out to be the beginning of a very unusual but sincere friendship. He was a retired bank inspector, who brought the fear of God into staff, when he turned up at a particular branch for an inspection. He was a confirmed bachelor - rather lonely, I suspect - and I was the latest in a long line of curates he had befriended, even though he was a worshipper at Bethania Chapel, in Mountain Ash. He pretended not to have much time for religion, but as I got to know him better, I knew that was just a front: deep down he was a very kind, generous, sincere and devoted man.

One such curate that he had befriended was from nearby Aberdare and was later to become a bishop of Bangor. I was visiting Cliff one day, enjoying a rather large glass of whisky, when in walked Tony Crocket - he was as surprised to see me as I was him, and we both ended up the worse for wear; I only had to crawl home, but he had to call a taxi.

Cliff was an outrageous character and didn't really care, in retirement, what he said. Here are some of his sayings:

On the wedding anniversary of a couple he knew: "They've been piddling in the same pot for forty years."

As I was coming out of his house one day, a parishioner was passing up the street; she was a spinster and had been a school-teacher, who had actually taught Val at Sunday school. She exclaimed: "I hope you are not corrupting our new curate, Mister Scurlock!" in her deep, school-ma'am voice.

"Oh, dear me, no, Miss Early - I wouldn't dream of doing such a thing!"

After she had passed by, he said: "She will be returned to her maker unopened."

She turned around; "Well, really, Mister Scurlock!"

When confronted by situations he had no control over, he would come out with one of the following:

"I couldn't give two tits in Taiwan..." or:

"I couldn't give two shits in Shanghai..." or, if he was really peeved:

"I couldn't give two fucks in Flanders…"

Here are some more of Cliff's sayings:

"We're all in a groove. The only difference between a groove and a grave is death."

"With regard to children, I love them and I'd love to have them, but I couldn't put up with their mothers."

"For the transient joys of this and that, is anything worth the fuss we make?"

"I get good days and bad days. I've got a feeling that the day after I was born was a good day; from then on it's been jet-black all the way, yet I persist in living."

"I must go now and have some spiritual benediction from Bell's (whisky)… and I'll clang it like hell!"

"I've got a feeling my psychology has gone adrift."

"He is colourless, clueless and humourless."

"He's got more foreskin than foresight."

"The best part of him trickled down his mother's legs."

Well, there you have it. Some of these sayings are quite near the mark, but I feel they are worth recording. He came out with them regularly, which is why I can remember them as if it were yesterday. Sadly, as he was a bachelor, whose family and friends are probably all gone now, I'm likely to be the only person who has made a copy of these outrageous sayings.

When Bishop Stephen was arrested for soliciting in public toilets, causing a huge scandal in the Church in Wales and beyond, Cliff's comment was: "A standing cock knows no conscience."

Mountain Ash, 1974

'I will instruct you and teach you in the way which you should go; I will counsel you with My eye upon you.'
Psalms 32:8

Father Gwilym said: "I want you to take the Sacrament to a family for me - I've got a hospital appointment about my back problems and I don't want to cancel that, or the home visit."

"No problem," I said, "just give me the details."

The family was the spinster sisters of the late Dr. Howell Pearce, who lived at Bryncerdin House. I arrived at the time arranged and rang the doorbell. A maid came to the door in a black outfit, complete with white ruff collar and a white cap, rather like a nurse would wear. I was a bit taken aback but stated my business, explaining that the vicar was indisposed. I was shown into the rather grand hall and told: "Sit there and I will tell Missus Pearce that you are here."

I sat and looked around at all the silver, bone-china ornaments and the portraits; I was lost in wonder, when a door opened and the maid said: "This way please - Missus Pearce will see you now."

They were very sweet and delighted to welcome me into their rather grand home. After I had given them Holy Communion, Miss Gwen said: "Do sit down, curate, and we shall have some refreshment."

Miss Dylis rang a bell and very soon the maid appeared with a silver tray, silver teapot, bone-china cups and some cucumber sandwiches; the sandwiches were so small that they contained just one slice of cucumber, peeled, and no crusts. I thought: *This is like an episode from* Pride and Prejudice - *I've been swept back in time, just by entering that front door.*

They were very interested in my life, especially that I had worked in a steelworks, and talking about my experiences with these two genteel ladies seemed, all of a sudden, very bizarre. After quite some time they bade me farewell and reminded me to offer their best wishes to the vicar.

Talking of genteel ladies, another "old girl" I used to visit was Miss Long. Once again, I had to put on my best new curate's voice and spend time with this delightful lady, who didn't enjoy good health. She didn't have a maid, alas, so I was left in the front room, while she went off to make tea. As she was walking down the hallway, I distinctly heard her say to herself: "Oh, isn't he handsome?"

Oh, I thought, *you've scored there, Rob!*

Once again, tea was served, with a silver tea service and bone-china cups; salmon sandwiches this time, but again no crusts. What's so wrong with crusts?

Miss Gladys Lewis used to regularly invite me to afternoon tea. She was a retired schoolmistress and was very excited about my forthcoming ordination to the priesthood. It is here that I met Miss Jessie Evans on a number of occasions, and both of them decided they were going to give me a gift: Jessie was going to pay for a purple stole, which I still use for funerals to this day, in Wales; Gladys gave me a carriage clock, which has sadly lost its way, through the passages of time.

You might be thinking that the parish of Mountain Ash is solely populated by elderly spinsters! Well, it isn't, of course, but it certainly has had its share of gentry and highly-respected people in society.

Mountain Ash, 1976

'A time to weep, and a time to laugh; a time to mourn, and a time to dance.'
Ecclesiastes 3:4

"Put *Big Spender* on and we'll dance together," said my friend, Linda.

On it goes, blaring out in my small, curate's house - what will the neighbours think? Well, Edie next door was a dear lady, but stone-deaf, so I was safe. Perhaps my reputation wasn't, though, by this time, after partying at least once a month. *Big Spender* blared out, and the last thing I remembered was that Linda and I ended up dancing in my bathroom, then we just slid down the wall together, in a drunken heap, as you do!

Sadly, in retirement, all these years later, I had to conduct the funeral rites for Linda. She would have been pleased, I think, that someone who knew her had conducted her service.

We had such fun in those days, holding parties in each other's houses - about six, in all, would see us through the year. What I remember most, though, before the drink set in, was Linda's sister, Val. I knew that she was the one for me, but I was a bit shy with girls, so I knew I had to work on that. Would she be the one? Who knew…?

We got engaged and exchanged rings, sitting in my wreck of a car. It was big news in the parish, that the curate was engaged to Edward Thomas the chemist's daughter - celebrations galore and a date was fixed for 2nd July 1977, at St. Margaret's.

At the engagement party, in Val's Mum's house to celebrate, a gentleman walked in, who became known to me as Uncle Hywel - he was Val's godfather. He said to Val: "You had to be different to everyone else, didn't you? I don't know!"

The bishop sent for me and declared that I would have to leave the parish, as it was not appropriate to stay in the town, after marrying a local girl. I was to be sent to the parish of Coity, with Nolton.

We went to see the house. It was in a field near the church and graveyard, but it was a wonderful first home - we loved it.

We have many happy memories of the parish and the house, and the young people we met became such good friends to us. Two of those are now priests; they were brothers: Martyn and Robert.

Their father came to me once and said: "What have you done? You've taken my boys away from the chapel, to your church."

I said: "Well, at least now they're part of the true faith." I moved out of the way, quickly, before he clonked me with his newspaper.

Our wedding was a wonderful occasion. Lots of parishioners came to watch, and my rector from Neath, who was now Dean of Llandaff, together with our vicar, Gwilym, took the ceremony between them. The wedding reception was in Ysguborwen Country House, which is now a nursing home (should have put our names down then). It was a splendid affair and between both sets of family and friends there were more there than I could count. However, Val's mum had kept an account of everything: who sat where, the menu, the invitation list, etc. We found these when we were clearing her house, after her death. My cousin's husband, Peter, was my best man and in the reception his opening words were that there were so many dog collars present, it was like Crufts!

The time came for our "going away". We changed in a room upstairs, then into the car, which had been duly decorated. Off we drove to Fishguard - the Abergwain Hotel - recommended by Cliff Scurlock, now a dear friend; the car broke down on the way! Such a different experience to youngsters' today, with their "stag dos" abroad and package holidays to exotic places - it was luxury to us; the car was fixed and got us to the hotel. Then, we moved on to Val's mum and dad's chalet in Freshwater East, for the rest of the honeymoon.

At the end of our honeymoon, we travelled to our first home in Coity. I took up my duties the next day.

God works in a mysterious way and I believe he has led us together. Val will never know how much she means to me and how she has been a pillar of strength and support throughout my ministry - I couldn't have done it without her. As a faithful church-going girl, brought up in the life of the parish, although she says she didn't really know what to expect, she nevertheless embraced it, as part of her new life with me. Her musical ability, love of liturgy and good church practices, and her understanding of how to deal with awkward people (coming from her experiences as a teacher), have been part of that pillar of support. Even now, in retirement, and in sunny Spain, we have that shared understanding of how things should be.

Coity, 1977

'His anger lasts a moment; his favour all through life. At night therefore tears but joy comes with the dawn.'
Psalms 30:5

Our marital home in the village of Coity, in the parish of Coity with Nolton, Bridgend, was wonderful. We both loved the house - it had lovely sized rooms, was situated near to the church, had a graveyard over the back wall, a pub and some beautiful walks.

The pub…

"Martyn, I could be arrested, you know, or get into deep trouble! You're underage - your parents would kill me if they knew you were in here with us."

"Oh, don't worry," says Mart: "I'll simply go out through the toilet window and jump over the wall, into my garden, if the police should come." The fact that his house was literally next door to the pub was even more scary, when thinking about his parents.

The fact that he's now a priest, a canon and serving in an exclusive Vale of Glamorgan parish, is amazing. His brother is the priest in Aberdare, where we now live in retirement.

On a Wednesday evening, after trying to learn bell-ringing, we would always end up in the Six Bells, appropriately named after our bell-tower. Val and I were so lucky: being young, we were surrounded by a gang of youngsters, all our age, who were not only bell-ringers but servers, choristers and good friends. We had such a wonderful time in that gorgeous parish - it will always hold a special place in our hearts, with so many special memories.

I was 27 and Val was 21. We were married just a week when, the day after we moved in, a lady knocked on the door and asked if Val would like to join the Sewing Guild. I went to ask her and she whispered: "I can't sew."

I returned to the front door, wondering how to word this, and decided to say that once we were settled and knew what commitments we had, she would let her know.

The next day, the rector's wife called and asked if she would like to join the Mothers' Union. I once again went to the back of the house and conveyed this invitation, to which Val whispered: "But, I'm not a mother!" I returned to the front door with the same explanation I gave to Mrs. Mixam.

Alas, it couldn't be ignored - eventually she joined the M.U. As for the Sewing Guild, well, one of the choristers/bell-ringers - whose name was also Val - said she would join if my Val joined. They did, and I think they mostly spent their time making tea, picking up bits and rewinding rolls of cotton, etc.

The rector consulted me, with regard to having another assistant curate join us. We met Christopher - along with two others - and his gregarious personality outshone the others; David actually went along with my choice! Would I regret this…? David said that he felt it was good to have someone of the same age, with similar things in common.

One day, just before his ordination, Chris knocked on our door and came in, full of fun and nonsense, as always, and asked a favour: would we put up one of his friends for the night, who wanted to come to his ordination? We agreed, of course. Her name was Doreen, she was easy to get along with, loved cats (we had two) and would be no trouble. No problem, we said.

On the way out, when at the garden gate, he turned and, with a huge grin, said: "Oh, I forgot to say: Doreen is a nun!"

I thought, then: *This boy is going to be a handful!*

Fortunately, Sister Doreen was a wonderful character and we fell in love with her, remaining friends until her death. She was of the Community of Saint Denis, in Warminster, and always came with gifts - they were second-, third- or even fourth-hand gifts, given to the community, but still we treasured them - they were priceless; to this day, my granddaughter has a small teddy bear, given to her dad by Sister Doreen. We went to Doreen's funeral in Warminster, and it was very moving to see a bunch of daisies on her coffin - just beautiful.

Chris was a great character and we got on well but, oh my goodness, he lacked a certain amount of seriousness with regard to his commitments. He was late for Morning Prayer nearly every day.

In the end, David said: "Is there something you can do about this?" looking at me with a grin on his face, as if to say: "Well, *you* chose him."

The solution was to ring Chris when I got up in the morning, then go to his house to pick him up, so we could arrive together at St. Mary's Nolton, for Morning Prayer. Very often, after ringing him when I awoke, by the time I arrived at his house, he'd gone back to sleep... this made us *both* late. Sometimes, he would actually put his cassock on over his pyjamas!

Fortunately, it was the custom for each curate to recite Evening Prayer in their own church, and there were only two churches, so Chris opted to join me. If he made it on time it was a plus, and if he never turned up, I insisted he recite it privately, at home; I was, after all, the senior curate (I promised not to tell the rector).

One day, he rang me to say he was stuck at a friend's house, because his car had broken down. It was his day off and he had stayed at his friend's the night before. He was desperate to get home without incurring expense as, of course, we curates were always broke.

"Can you tow me home? My friend has got a tow-rope."

"Well, I suppose so, although I'm a bit anxious about doing that. Where are you?"

"Blackmill."

"Blackmill?"

"Yes."

"Bloody-hell, you're nuts! I can't tow you all the way from Blackmill."

"It'll be alright - don't worry."

"I have to be at Bridgend Leisure Centre at two p.m., for a meeting."

"Plenty of time - you can drop me off there."

"What about the car? You can't leave it there – you'll be clamped!"

"*I'll* worry about that."

"Yes, I bet."

The tow-rope, which had seen better days, broke three times on the way home. We made it to the car park of the leisure centre, in Bridgend town centre, and parked his car behind mine, then he got into my car for us to decide what to do next.

One of our parishioners was a garage mechanic, so it was simply a case of contacting him to come and pick the car up. We didn't have his address to hand, and these were the days before mobile phones, so we knew he would have to wait until my meeting was over, before consulting the parish electoral roll and ringing this guy from my house.

Just then, a car pulled up beside mine.

"It's the rector," I said.

"What the hell is he doing here?"

"He's going to the same meeting as me, with the mayor, about the forthcoming civic service."

"Can you believe he's parked next to us?"

By this time we were on the floor of the car, praying he wouldn't see us. However, Christopher was giggling like an idiot! Fortunately, the rector didn't see us, and we dared to raise our heads after a while – we caught sight of him, behind the huge glass windows, climbing the stairs inside the leisure centre, to the meeting upstairs. We vacated my car; Chris on foot, to his home, and me to join the rector at the meeting.

A TIME TO WEEP AND A TIME TO LAUGH

Mountain Ash/Coity, 1979

'He heals the broken-hearted, he binds up all their wounds.' Psalms 147:3

We were visiting Val's mum and dad, it was a Saturday and there was an international rugby match in the afternoon. After a splendid lunch, as always, waiting for the match to begin, it started snowing.

Val's Mum was immediately anxious, as we had quite a journey home to Coity, but we both said that it would probably come to nothing, as usual. In the end though, we could see that perhaps we should go, in case we got stuck in Mountain Ash and I would be unable to celebrate Mass the following day, causing chaos in the parish - we both felt confident that we would drive out of it. After saying our goodbyes, we left.

It seemed to be fine and I felt confident that by the time we got to the Coryton roundabout, it would fizzle out. Then, turning off the roundabout and on to the M4, we had hardly travelled a hundred yards, before things changed, drastically - it was as if we had left Wales and immediately entered Switzerland! It was the M4 corridor, as they call it, and as we progressed, the snow became a severe blizzard, the signs flashed "30", then a little later "20", then "10", then "5" miles per hour - I started to panic that the next sign flashing at us would say "STOP!" Fortunately, by a miracle, we crawled off the motorway and made our way to the village of Coity, and I actually managed to get the car into the garage. As fresh snow was falling at an alarming rate, it was actually easier to drive over than the snow impacted by previous cars.

When we arrived home, I phoned my mum to make sure she was okay...

No reply... Panic... Was she alright?

I phoned Sue, my cousin, who informed us that there was very little snow in Neath, and that she was probably at Auntie Nancy's.

We realized there would probably be no church in the morning, but if it melted overnight, then I could get up early in the morning and put things ready for the few who turned up.

In the morning, we couldn't see out: the snow was covering the downstairs windows. It had drifted, so some parts were completely inaccessible while other parts could be walked along. Thanks to trees and walls, the drift allowed me to make my way from the house to the church - which took ages - and inside there were at least two inches of snow covering everything. It was eerie... The heating had failed to come on, too - it was freezing! Martyn and Robert turned up and we decided to celebrate Mass in my study.

It was like an enforced bank holiday for the best part of the week, roads only becoming accessible gradually, as each day passed. Bell-ringers congregated on the Tuesday and we walked up to the farm belonging to Valerie Pearce's family - Valerie was one of our bell-ringing group. We were determined to do this, not only for the fun of it, but also to make sure she and her family were okay. We were literally walking on top of the hedgerows. Later in the week we were able to make our way to Litchard, and on Litchard hill saw the most enormous snow-drift - newspapers later reported it as being nineteen-feet high. It caused chaos in Bridgend for quite a while, but the fellowship it created between us youngsters in the village - with regular visits to the Six Bells (the pub, not the tower) - is a time I will always remember, fondly. In fact, I have always loved snow, and this experience was a dream come true for me.

One Sunday morning, I could see a couple sitting half-way down the aisle, and noted that they were new faces – either visitors on holidays, relatives of parishioners, or maybe even newcomers. There was something about the man staring at me all the time that made me uneasy.

I made a mental note to get to the back of the church and greet them, before they rushed off, however, with all the fuss of shaking hands, greeting people and listening to important information, I looked around, and to my dismay they were gone. I could remember their faces and looked down the church path to see if I could run after and welcome them, but alas, there was no sign of them. *How odd,* I thought: *they must have scarpered very quickly.* I spoke to the wardens - they recalled the couple, but couldn't remember them shooting off, either.

It was years later, when the solicitor in Eastbourne gave me bits and pieces from my father, among them photographs, that I recognized him; I am wholeheartedly convinced that my father and Elsie had visited St. Mary's Church that day - he was obviously as curious about me as I was about him. No wonder they scurried off, not wishing to become engaged in conversation with me. If I had known they were coming, I would have prepared a special homily... maybe themed on parental love!

One day, a publisher contacted me out of the blue, offering *The World Book of Donkins*; I was intrigued! It wasn't very expensive, so I sent off for it. When it arrived, I scoured all the addresses in the Newcastle and Tyne area - where he was born - and also Eastbourne, of course. I wrote to these people, explaining who I was, my father's name and details, in the hope that he or some other relative would answer.

I had only one reply, which didn't make any sense, and I thought it was some nutter! Foolishly, I discarded the letter and all I can remember now about one part of the content was an unusual sentence or two, mentioning that "it isn't always wrong to be at a distance". I am convinced now that it was Elsie, who had received my letter and, in perhaps a slightly demented state of mind, had written. If only I had kept that letter, I could have checked the handwriting, years later in Aberaman, against Elsie's letter, on behalf of my father. Don't throw anything out!

Pontrhydyfen, 1981

'So the Lord was with Joshua; and his fame was in all the land.' Joshua 6:27

"Guess who I've just met."

"No idea", says Val.

"None other than Richard Burton."

"Pigs might fly!"

"I'm not kidding. I was walking down Penhydd Street to visit Nancy, when I saw a big black car; I thought there might have been a death, as it looked like a funeral car. Bill came out of his house and I asked him whose it was.

"'Oh, it's Rich's.'

"'Rich? Who is Rich?'

"'Richard Burton'.

"'You're joking!'

"'No. Come and meet him.'

"'Oh, heck, I can't do that - he'll think I'm silly!'

"'No, he won't. And, Hilda will be mad if she knows you were on the street and didn't call.'"

I was terrified, but Bill dragged me into Hilda's house to meet her famous brother and his new wife. She proudly ushered me into the front room, where he sat with Sally Bowles - wife number... can't remember. He was charming and very interested in the life of the Church in the village. A rather large glass of whisky was thrust into my hand by Hilda and I couldn't quite believe what was happening. I thought: *Nobody is going to believe me when I tell them!*

There were other famous people from Pontrhydyfen, one of whom is a very dear friend: Rebecca Evans, now an international opera singer.

One character in the village was called Blod: short for Blodwyn. On one of my visits to her she told me how humble Rich was and, surprisingly, Elizabeth Taylor, too. They used to walk hand in hand through the village (my parish!) - two international superstars! They would visit the local shops and catch up on the gossip; they would often end up in the Post Office and chat with Betty and Howard, Rebecca Evans's parents - how ironic that, years later, I would do the same, sitting possibly in the same seat. Rich and Liz would inevitably end up in The Miner's Arms, after their walk through the village.

Blod related a story that was very dear to her: she had been on a Wallace Arnold bus-tour to Italy; they had reached Rimini, which was part of their itinerary, however, they found themselves in a traffic jam. The bus driver was becoming more and more annoyed at the delay - he got out of the bus and came back a little later, with the news:

"Oh, it's Richard Burton and Elizabeth Taylor – they're on their yacht in the bay and the press are waiting until they come ashore."

Blod shrieked: "I know him - he's from my village. I know them both!"

After roars of laughter from the other passenger, she

exclaimed, again: "I'm going out there now and see what's going on. I know him, see?"

More laughter...

"Rich! Rich!" shouted Blod, from the quayside. "Rich! Rich, it's Blod, from Pontrhydyfen."

"Who is it?" said Richard.

"It's Blod, from Pontrhydyfen!"

Elizabeth Taylor said to him: "It's got to be somebody you know, as they are calling you 'Rich'!"

Richard listened more intently then, with binoculars, identified Blod; "I'll send a small boat over for you, Blod."

He did indeed and, on his million-dollar yacht, Blod sat sipping champagne, with two dear friends that she knew so well. The tour bus had to park somewhere, and the passengers crowded at the quayside, not quite believing their eyes.

As she told me, once: "I helped bring him up, see?" How Welsh is that?!

Hilda, his sister, told me once that buses often used to park outside the house, whilst the driver explained all about Richard Burton's birthplace. A view from that street took in a number of important landmarks relating to his life. On one occasion, a bus pulled up and she was in the front room, so she went out to speak to them.

The driver apologized and said: "I'm sorry, Missus Owen - I just wanted to show these folks where your brother hailed from." It was a small thirty-seater.

Hilda said: "Come on in and I'll make you all a cup of tea."

How Welsh is that?!

They couldn't resist - they filled the house and tea and biscuits were served... But... who was making the tea in the back kitchen? None other than Elizabeth Taylor, on a quick visit, while Rich was meeting producers, to talk about a film version of Dylan Thomas's *Under Milk Wood*.

Pontryhdyfen, 1981

'Truly children are a gift from the Lord, a blessing, the fruit of the womb.'
Psalms 127:3

I knocked on Hilda's front door, on the way home from the hospital. She was up in no time at all, no doubt expecting a call. After all, Val had gone into labour the day before and we were all on red alert.

I said: "You have a beautiful, blond, baby grandson."

"Oh, my angel baby!" she said, not talking about me, of course - even though she hadn't seen my beautiful blond, baby bombshell yet.

Symon changed our lives - we adored him and still do. He was a wonderful baby, and so easy to care for. The villagers of Pontryhyfen adored him, too; such a famous village to be born in. Pontrhydyfen was the birthplace of actor Richard Burton, Broadway theatre, musical star Ivor Emmanuel (who was also in *Zulu*), international opera singer Rebecca Evans (a personal friend), Welsh singer and songwriter Geraint Griffiths and actor Mark Frankel. The "Richard Burton Appreciation Society" is based in the village.

The churchwarden's wife, Eleri, took great pride in collecting Symon and pushing him, in his pram, through the village, telling everyone that this was the vicar's little baby boy. I understand that he spent quite a lot of time on these trips in the Post Office which, at the time, was managed by Betty and Howard, the parents of Rebecca Evans. There, he had quite an audience.

Hilda, my mum, had a tendency to "say it like it is", and we nearly died of embarrassment one Sunday morning, when we heard a stage whisper: "He's too good for this place." She was referring to me, having obviously felt that I had outgrown a small Welsh village parish, in spite of its fame.

We met some wonderful characters there and I often used to think of scenes from *Under Milk Wood*, as I exercised my ministry there.

Two years later, my beautiful darling daughter Rebecca was born. When Hilda came to the hospital to visit, I placed Rebecca in her arms. She immediately started to cry and Hilda said: "Oh, come on now, you cheeky little thing!"

To which I said: "She's following you."

That expression has borne itself out in many ways, not only in looks but tendencies - it's all in the genes, as we say. If Hilda came into a room, where Val and I had poured a drink for each other, with hands on her hips she would say: "Indeed!" as if we were excluding her. We weren't, of course - just waiting for her to arrive. One day, in Penarth, Rebecca came downstairs into the kitchen, where we were enjoying a glass of wine; lo and behold, with hands on her hips, she said: "Indeed!"

Then, of course, whenever Becky packs to go away, everything is laid out on the bed first, then carefully put into the suitcase - I wonder where she gets that from: Hilda Donkin?

When Val's mum came to the hospital, she brought a

strange bunch of flowers. As it was a bank holiday weekend, she had bought flowers and put them in the freezer, ready for the announcement of the birth. They didn't defrost too well, and when the nurses came around, in turn they would say: "Shall I get rid of those for you, love?"

Val always replied: "No, my mother brought them for me." The expression on the nurses' faces was priceless.

Both children have made us so very proud, Symon being a capable carpenter, securing a good job and getting himself on the property market at twenty years of age - the age I was in college; he is so able to get on with things.

Rebecca, after travelling the world, secured a job with the Welsh National Opera Company, later with the Glyndbourne Opera Company, then back to the W.N.O., as Chorus Manager. She, too, had a property of her own, in exclusive Cardiff Bay, but has now sold that and bought a three-bedroom house near us. There are a number of heavenly bodies looking down, plucking their harps with pride.

It was here, in Pontryhdyfen, that I began to realize that I wanted more from my daily prayer life than just Morning and Evening Prayer - it came with my second outpouring of the Holy Spirit. I was in church, tidying up, and instinctively I felt the need to recite something. I realized it was midday and it came to me that this was the hour of the crucifixion. I took the prayer book and recited psalms, sang a hymn, offered a reading and the collect for the day; I had, in fact, recited an Office.

When I mentioned this to my Spiritual Director of the time, he quickly advised me that I should use the Roman Divine Office.

I bought a shortened version – *Daily Prayer* - to see how I got on with it. I couldn't wait to have the full set and, over a period of time, managed to acquire them as birthday or anniversary presents. It is a fantastically composed sanctifying of the day and has enriched my priestly life ever since.

Pontrhydyfen, 1981

'The souls of the righteous are in the hands of God and no torment will ever touch them.'
Wisdom 3:9

"Oh, I peed myself soaking, Vicar - I've never laughed so much in my life!"

I cannot remember what she was laughing at, because I was so taken by surprise at her comment - a comment she would make regularly, at many an event!

She was Doris*, the landlady of the Colliers Arms in Efail Fach, a hamlet between the hamlet of Pontrhydyfen and the village of Tonmawr. It was, in fact, the parish of Oakwood, just to confuse you. In the village of Oakwood stood the parish church, then next came the hamlet of Pontrhydyfen (but don't tell them it's that!); next along was the hamlet of Efail Fach, then came the village of Tonmawr. The point is that if a village does not have a church then it is a hamlet - it is only a village or town if it has a church.

So, it was in the Colliers Arms in Efail Fach that I arranged with Doris to have the reception, following the baptism of my newly born blond-bombshell son, Symon. The baptism went well, with Symon's godfather - a very dear friend - taking part. Parishioners came to support, and my mother and Val's mother were proud grandparents. Val's Dad, Edward, took it all in his stride, though enjoyed the reception in the Colliers very much - the reception was phenomenal!

What a unique place that was, and what a fascinating family. Here follow some treasures from my memory of that place:

One winter we had quite a substantial fall of snow, and I was concerned about my mother - who lived over the hill in the next parish, of Neath, where I was born, in the area of Cimla - so I ventured over to see her on foot. I needn't have worried: she was fine and had plenty of provisions. After a while I made my way back to Pontrhydyfen, but was enticed by the tempting glow from the Colliers Arms. So, I succumbed and ventured in, only to receive a wonderful welcome from Bryn and Doris.

After about half an hour I had drunk two whiskies, the trouble being there were four more on the bar in front of me, bought by men in the pub. I was taken aback that anyone felt that moved to buy me a whisky... or four. Of course, it would be unthinkable to leave them there, and I got through them, enjoyably.

I decided it was time to get back to the vicarage, and one man, who lived near us, asked me how I was getting home. I told him that I had been visiting my mother because of the snow and that I would walk the rest of the way through the village. He offered to give me a lift. I sort of hesitated, because he had surely drunk more than me. However, Doris said: "Go on, Vicar, you'll be fine - he's not as pissed as you."

It was snowing heavily and I thought: *Well, if this is the end, so be it!*

We got into his car. By this time the main road was barely

visible – the mounds on either side of the road were once cars! I thought that soon we would have to abandon the car and walk, as the car crawled through the village and made it to the famous Pontrhydyfen aqueduct. It was no longer used for water, thank God, but had been tarmacked over, many years ago, to provide vehicle access to Oakwood, where we lived; thus, it was now the Pontrhydyfen viaduct. I thought surely here we would need to walk. Not so... not so... my chauffeur put his foot down...!

We sled – yes, *sled* - through the viaduct, which by now had become like a toboggan-race route in the Olympic games - the car actually swerved from side to side, touching the walls of the aqueduct, which were now thick with snow... just like the games.

We made it home.

Doris, Bryn and their family suffered much tragedy. First to hit them was the death of their seventeen-year-old son, Tony - he died in a road-traffic accident. I was very traumatized to have to comfort the family, organize the funeral and eventually conduct the funeral rites. They were a very close-knit family and welcomed me into their midst, as if I were part of the family. The day of the funeral was horrendous, and I was still a young priest, and rather inexperienced with such tragedies, at the age of thirty. I could not help but admire the courage of Doris and Bryn. They took me to their hearts, in spite of my immature dealings with them.

On one occasion, I popped into the Colliers to visit Bryn and Doris, just to see how they were doing, and who should be there but our local G.P. Lott. He was quite a character, as were all his family. On one occasion, I needed a consultation with him in his surgery, which required me lowering my pants. After a routine investigation, he said: "There's nothing wrong there, Vic - you can get dressed."

Anyway, back to the Colliers...

If the vicar was a celebrity in the village, then the local doctor was even more so. When I popped in, on one occasion, I had the usual wonderful welcome and a whisky was thrust into my hand, before I could say: "Hello." At the bar was Dr. Lott, with a whisky, bought by a grateful patient. By the time I joined him I had another whisky in front of me also, as well as the one I held in my hand.

Although we were interrupted all night by people wanting medical advice and religious counselling, we did have a great night; I think we both went home with a deeper understanding of both our vocations.

Later, I was to bury Roy, who was Bryn and Doris's eldest son. I had the call late one night, and couldn't believe the message I was hearing on my phone. I quickly got my act together and made my way to the Colliers.

I prayed, as I always do in tragic circumstances: "Please God, give me the words to say."

What *was* I going to say to this family, after their previous tragedy? The second of their sons, dead!

When I got there, Doris was strong, but Bryn was in tears on my shoulder, like a small boy. I couldn't make any arrangements with him, but Doris knew exactly what she wanted. We made some initial notes and arranged for me to come back in the morning.

Roy was gay and lived with his partner, Evan. That was quite avant-garde in those days: to be openly gay and living together, yet nobody cared. Evan drove coaches for a local bus company and I knew them both - they were lovely characters. They lived in a fabulous bungalow which Bryn had built for them. Everyone in the village knew the circumstances, but it didn't bother anyone, and nobody spoke about it - least of all the family, who loved Roy and Evan to bits.

Once again, the funeral was horrendous and took all of my skills, as a young priest, to deal with.

Not only was my blond bombshell of a baby boy, Symon, baptized in Pontrhydyfen, but my beautiful baby girl was also born and baptized there.

To be parishioner-friendly, having had Symon's celebration in St. John's, Oakwood, we decided to have Rebecca's in Tonmawr. This went down well - that the vicar's little girl was going to be baptized in Tonmawr - and it made everyone very pleased. Needless to say, the reception was held in the Colliers, with the same aplomb we had for Symon. Bryn and Doris were so generous - I feel sure that the final bills for both celebrations were a lot less than they should have been.

Alas, later in life, in the parish of Aberaman, I had a phone call to say that Bryn had died. I couldn't believe how much poor Doris had already suffered.

They wanted me to do the funeral. As the parish was in

interregnum, it was easy to arrange for me to return and help this poor family, yet again, especially as I had only recently left.

There was one brighter incident, in the middle of all these tragedies: Terry, their middle son, was getting married, and the family invited Val and myself. He was a lovely lad and he and his gorgeous bride were married in a chapel; after the ceremony the reception was held in an exclusive hotel in Newport.

The gap between the actual ceremony and the wedding reception was quite lengthy - this resulted in far too many drinks; I can't even remember what we drank. When the food was eventually served it slipped down, unnoticed, and before we could return home we had to stop for fish and chips, we were so desperately hungry. As for driving under the influence, I don't think breathalyzers had really made their impact in those days!

**Name changed to protect identity.*

Aberaman, 1983

'You did not choose me but I chose you. And I appointed you to go and bear fruit.'
John 15:16

"Oh, hell - that's ridiculous! I'm not going there," I said, in a rebellious fit.

"What's the matter?" said Val.

"They want me to go to the parish of Aberaman and Abercwmboi!"

This is all because I dared to apply for another parish, which then sent out the message that I was looking for a move. I wrote and refused, saying that it was too difficult for Val to travel to her school, that it was too near my former parish of Mountain Ash and that Val's family, who lived in the next parish of Mountain Ash, might be embarrassed if I were ever to be seen as that vicar who changed everything. You know how it is! I posted the letter and waited for a reply.

I received a phone call instead: the archdeacon, once described by one of my churchwardens as a "boring old fart". He persuaded me to apply, saying that he could even get Val a job in a church-school. He said it needed some T.L.C., as the previous incumbent had introduced some very interesting ways - being a foreign gentleman, he had brought some strange habits. On his first Sunday, he had announced that it was the custom in his country for the priest to receive gifts from his flock - he said the vicarage would be opened the next day for this purpose. One lady said to me that there was no racial prejudice in this parish until "that foreign gentleman" came!

We chewed it over, and overriding our decision was the teaching drummed into me that "you go where you are sent", even if it was not by the bishop but a "boring old fart"!

We went to look at the parish and were gob-smacked to understand that we would have to live in a sixteen-roomed mansion! There was a linen-room, which I quickly turned into an oratory for my personal devotions, there was a butler's room, which had been converted into a utility room and a maid's pantry, converted into a boiler-room; the scullery had been converted into a kitchen and the kitchen into a breakfast-room. The dining room featured a long table, created from two old tables, by a former priest; it sat sixteen of us comfortably, at Christmas and other family occasions. When he was naughty, I used to chase Symon up the servants' staircase, along the servants' quarters and down the main staircase, which was a very grand affair. My churchwarden of blessed memory used to comment that she could imagine a bride coming down those stairs, ready for her wedding.

I hasten to add that the servants had long gone, although there was a very dear lady in the congregation, who had been the last live-in nursery-maid. I felt it was a pity she was too old to take over again, with the running of a huge household and two small children. Val did go back to work and we could only manage this because of two special characters in the parish:

Audrey and Brin. With my mother deceased, they took her place, and along with Granny and Grandad, in Glenboi, we coped. I always used to think that they still had two sets of grandparents - their real ones in Glenboi and surrogate ones in Aberaman, replacing Hilda and Georgie-Porgie-Pudding-and-Pie; the children loved Auntie Audrey and Uncle Brin, and they were the sort of people whom we could trust to take over and supervise the children, whenever needed... and that was often!

St. Margaret's Church had been built by Sir George Elliot, in memory of his wife, Margaret. Good job her name wasn't "Esmeralda", and that there are saints named Margaret, I used to say. He was the local owner of the coalmines and collieries, providing employment for thousands. He built the vicarage, but declared that it should not be bigger than his own house, Aberaman House. Thank God it wasn't - in those days, he provided the coal to heat the sixteen rooms, and paid for the servants; come back, Sir George - all is forgiven! However, the parish was extremely generous and, after advice from the parsonage board, agreed they would pay the whole of the gas bill, if we would keep the thermostat low all day and night, and just put fires on in the rooms we were sitting in, during the evenings. This worked out cheaper for everybody and we will ever be grateful to the parish.

From Sir George's travels, there was a piece of the great pyramid of Giza, on the wall of the church. I still wonder if that could be auctioned and secure the Church in Wales's finances for the next century.

Here, the children grew up in the Faith and, with such a

wonderful congregation, we were given so much love and support, taking with us memories that we still cherish. It is something very wonderful that we have now retired back to that parish. We bought the house when it was situated outside my parish, but then Bishop Roy joined the parish of Cwmaman to the existing parish, and we suddenly found we had a house in my parish. However, it matters not now, all these years later, as there have been two priests since. It is wonderful to help out now, when the vicar is away, and see that things have progressed and grown, since my time in the parish. Many of the congregation that I knew and loved are still worshipping faithfully; it is such an inspiration, and they have a wonderful new priest, whom they love.

Perhaps it was because of such love and respect from the congregation, that the Lord saw fit to bless me with another outpouring of the Holy Spirit. I felt on fire again and it led me to several retreats at Ty Mawr, a retreat centre run by Benedictine nuns, near Monmouth. Here, I learnt to pray the Divine Office in its fullness, which has been the fundamental basis of my daily prayer, and still is. Here, also, I learnt to pray the Rosary, which is the most amazing way of surrounding family, friends and situations - domestic and global - with the life of Jesus. The Joyful, Sorrowful, Luminous and Glorious mysteries of this mystical way of praying embraces life situations and brings results! The celebration of Mass, of course, is the joy of my life, and my only sadness is that retirement means I haven't got an altar every day. This is why my ministry in Spain is such a gem in my life, especially thanks to our beloved Father Richard.

REV. CANON ROBERT DONKIN

Aberaman, 1984

'The Lord is close to the broken-hearted; those whose spirit is crushed he will save.'
Psalms 34:19

"Okay, Mum. Look after yourself now and we'll see you when we come back from Bournemouth.

"By the way, Rebecca has started walking."

"Oh, I'm going to miss that!"

"By the time we come home she'll be walking up the drive to meet you, don't worry." I put the phone down.

The next morning was spent walking around sixteen rooms, unplugging things, securing windows, checking on the heating, etc., then putting the children in the car, ready to set off for Bournemouth.

The phone goes...

"Oh, who's that now?" I said, irritably.

"Hi, Rob, it's Sue. I've got something to tell you... it's bad news - you need to sit down: your mother's dead."

Silence...

"She can't be - I only spoke to her last night!"

I was devastated, bewildered, heartbroken...! For all her faults, she was mother, father, brother, sister, best friend and much more. It took me a long time to get over it, mainly because people don't want to see the vicar crying, so I bottled it up. In fact, it took nearly two years to get over it, because I was foolish enough to do that.

The first year is when you brace yourself for the first of everything: first birthday, first Christmas, first Easter, first anniversary, without them. The second year is when it really sinks in and you realize they're gone. How people cope without a faith, I don't know. My "Born Again" experiences gave me the reassurance that she was watching over me.

Having watched my grandfather die, and seen him looking up towards the corner of the ceiling and smiling, made me aware then, as a young man, that they were beckoning him - *they* being the angels, gathered to greet him. Val had a similar experience when her dad died.

I often wonder if Mum and my father are reunited. Where Elsie would fit into that, I'm not quite sure - perhaps they would make a threesome!

The parish rallied around with such love. They were aghast that I should arrive in the parish as their new vicar, meet my mother, then mourn with me, just three months later. The churchwarden of blessed memory became like a mother, in many ways: she was reassuring and supportive of all that I did. She said to me, once: "You've left no stone unturned." This was such a compliment for all my hard work.

The not-unturned stones were, of course, my way of dealing with bereavement, and I became a workaholic. However, the Kingdom of God benefitted, because everything I tried to do was wonderfully supported, by such marvellous parishioners, that we seemed to go from strength to strength, with their love and undying help. The churchwarden of blessed memory has to be named here as Peggy Davies; she and her family were gems in parish life, and her son-in-law would soon offer himself for ordination - he became my first curate and a tremendous colleague. We still laugh and reminisce with joy, at our time together in Aberaman.

Aberaman, 1985

'We know that all things work together for good for those who love God, who are called according to his purpose.'
Romans 8:28

Sitting in the front of the hearse made one feel sort of "on show", a little bit. People would stare, some would take their caps off to show respect, some would make the sign of the cross, some would bow, but all would stop what they were doing; very few would ignore. Unlike the present day, unfortunately.

"Well, that went well, Vicar", said the undertaker. "Nice family - terrible loss for them."

"Yes, I know. I wonder if she'll stay there on her own", I said.

"Oh, I'm sure she will - wonderful neighbours and the family aren't far away.

"Now, see that grave there?"

"Which one (there were hundreds to be seen)?"

"That big, red granite one, there."

"Oh yes, I can see it."

"Well, he used to be the Fat Man in the fair, when it came to Aberdare."

"Really? We had a big fair come to Neath - it still does - and when I was a boy I knew the Fat Man: he came to our house to see my grandparents; when my grandfather kept a pub, he used to call in for his pints. He kept in touch, after the pub closed. I wonder if it's the same person."

"Well, after we've buried this coffin, we'll stop on the way back to see, shall we?"

"Oh, that would be great."

It was him, indeed: Mr. Lambert - such a lovely gentleman. So sad that he had to make a living by wearing a tiger skin and sitting for hours while people glared... and laughed! There are so many obese people today, he'd be one amongst thousands and never have a job! I have a photo of him. It was somehow very moving to stand there by his grave, and think of those days in the old house at Angel Street, formerly The Tiger. What a small world.

I suddenly felt very sad that my grandparents and Mum were all dead - I had no-one to tell; they would have been tickled pink that I had stood at his grave.

As happy as we were in Aberaman, there came a time when I felt more of a manager than a parish priest. In the Thatcher years there sprung up the Manpower Services Commission: organizations and churches were encouraged to be sponsors of a scheme which would bring employment and opportunities to those seeking work and experience. Well, a gentleman called to the vicarage one day and explained all this; I was very interested and put it all to the churchwardens and P.C.C. They decided to go for it. Indeed, the parish did well out of it and the end result was that the church, the crypt, the church-hall and surrounding grounds were all restored magnificently. The parish needed to find certain funds, which they did, loyally...

"Oh Lord, I can't go looking like this!"

"Well, you decided on a 'vicars and tarts' party to raise money for this scheme," said Val.

"I know, but I look like my mother!"

"Only facially - she didn't have plastic boobs protruding from her dress and she was certainly no tart!"

"Well, that's the doorbell, the first to arrive - there's no going back now!"

The evening was hilarious and we felt that it brought us together, as a parish family, in such a wonderful way. Alun Jones still threatens to produce photos of me dressed as a tart, all these years later! It has to be said that this event was a turning point for Bernard Jones, who was soon to offer himself for ordination and would become my N.S.M curate.

The day I realized I was becoming a manager and not a priest was when we were on holidays at Oxwich Bay and Ian, one of the assistant managers of the scheme in Aberaman, came running along the beach, while we were sunbathing (it was a small resort in Gower, and it wasn't difficult to find who you wanted on the beach) - he wanted me to sign an important document. I had thought by then that my privacy was destroyed and I had to go - unknown to anyone but Val and Bishop Roy, I had applied for a position as a hospital chaplain to two places: Welwyn Garden City and Chichester. I was short-listed for both and felt quite proud to have got that far in the process. I was glad that I didn't get the job in Welwyn Garden City, as we didn't really like the place at all. However, the interview at

Chichester was quite something.

"Now, we can see that you have many years of good experience, which will put you in good stead for a position here," said the manager.

"You have wonderful references, from two well-respected hospital chaplains," said a senior nurse.

"How do you feel you would cope in a crisis?"

Several scenarios were put before me and I had to explain how I would attend to a dying patient with AIDS, a train crash with multiple wounded, and a terrorist attack, with angry family members. I answered each question to the best of my ability and felt quite confident.

But, then, a clergyman from the diocese of Chichester asked me a question:

"Now, coming from Wales, how do you think you would cope, living in this beautiful area, with so much culture on offer?"

Perhaps for the first time in my life I was speechless, and weighed up how I should answer. I said: "Well, it will be a shock to the system, because *Wales* is such a beautiful country, with such a historical musical tradition and an abundance of culture. Our Christian heritage goes way back to the Celtic Church, which was truly Catholic, long before the Anglo-Saxons invaded with their Teutonic ways. So, yes, I will find it hard to live in a place like this, but I dare say I will tolerate it."

I knew that I had just lost my chance of the position - however, it had to be said. I just got up, smiled sweetly and said: "However, I don't think I would really want to live amongst such prejudice. Goodbye." The manager got to his feet and came to the door before I could leave, asking me to stay, but it was too late.

I realized that the Lord was sending me a clear message: I was needed in Llandaff, in the diocese that had trained and ordained me. I decided then to be loyal to it, and I think I was rewarded for it in later years, in my ministry. Bishop Roy was delighted.

I returned home, rejoicing, and was not surprised to receive a letter telling me that "unfortunately at this time" I was "unsuccessful in my application".

Well, my gain! I thought.

Aberaman, 1986

'But the souls of the righteous are in the hands of God.'
Wisdom 3:1

"Oh God, isn't she bloody beautiful, vicar? I wanted the coffin open, see, so that all the family could give her a final kiss, before the funeral tomorrow."

Oh God, I thought, *the quicker they screw her down the better, before there's an epidemic.*

The woman then kissed her mother's forehead and I prayed she wouldn't expect me to do the same. I quickly geared the family's thoughts to prayer, which is why I had been asked to call in the first place.

The following day was a typical Welsh valleys funeral. The first part was held in the house - I have always felt that there is something very beautiful and meaningful about that: to have prayers in the family home, where the deceased had lived, loved, nurtured etc., before the main funeral service takes place - either in church or the cemetery - is very symbolic. Thus, the service is held in the house, with all the family gathered around the coffin. Though it is hard to conduct a ceremony in circumstances like that - as you are close to the bereaved - the service went well in the house. I always used to position myself at the foot of the coffin and get the nearest and dearest to position themselves at the head, so I could focus on them with the liturgy and, especially, the eulogy.

In those days, the tradition of giving money to charity, in lieu of flowers, was a new concept - it would be some time before it would really take off; this meant there were floral tributes all over the lounge. The undertaker had asked me to consider that it could maybe take twenty minutes to remove the flowers and load up the car! Apparently, the biggest problem was a floral display in the shape of a chair. It was a magnificent specimen and couldn't be brought into the house, so it remained on the pavement.

After the service, I stepped out of the house to await the journey to the cemetery. Much discussion was to be heard regarding this "floral chair", and I couldn't help but hear some of the comments. One lady said: "Oh, God love her, they've brought her commode!"

We proceeded to the next part of the funeral, and I decided I would not look at the *chair*.

Aberaman, 1995

'Are any among you sick? They should call for the elders of the Church and have them pray over them, anointing them with oil in the name of the Lord.'
James 5:14

"You're looking a bit on fire, Vicar. Have you had too much sun?"

We were on our way home from Tenby - the Sunday School Annual Outing. It had been "a flaming June day", as Hilda would have said.

"I'm okay," I said.

The next morning I celebrated Mass, but struggled, and afterwards I was told that people could see this.

Later in the day, Val had to call for the "out of hours" doctor. He came and wondered if it was meningitis. I was rushed to hospital and given all the tests, but there was bewilderment. They then wondered if it was leukaemia, by which time I was beside myself. I was finally diagnosed with systemic lupus erithemetosis - or "S.L.E." - commonly just called "lupus". I was told to keep out of the sun and to use factor-50 sun-cream every day, even in cloud and rain. I was told to wear a hat always, never to go abroad and never to sunbathe!

I called for the chaplain, Steve Morgan. He anointed me with the oil of the sick and gave me the Blessed Sacrament.

When I returned home, I was told to see my local G.P. He admitted that he would have to do some research, as it was a rare disease, and made an appointment for me to see him the next day. When I returned the next day, he told me to make a will, that I would probably not live beyond fifty and would soon be confined to a wheelchair!

I contacted St. Luke's Hospital for the Clergy, in London. The consultant there felt there was no real evidence that I had lupus, but to err on the side of caution. Another consultant in Prince Charles Hospital, Merthyr Tydfil, said much the same.

That summer, we were due to take our caravan and the children to France, with Linda and Andrew - that had to be cancelled. However, Val towed the caravan and we managed a holiday in Devon. Setting up the caravan and awning, all of a sudden, I felt a surge pass through me; I felt stronger, and it occurred to me that whatever this disease was, it had left me. I gained strength daily, and by the time we returned home I wondered what was going on. I felt fine and ditched the sun-cream which made me look like Coco the Clown. Having ordered a Cure Da'r hat, from Barberini's in Rome, I wore it for a while, but decided it made me look too much like my mother; she would have loved the hat, being a milliner by trade.

By the time we had moved to Penarth, my new doctor was intrigued and not convinced that I had lupus. He sent me to Llandough hospital, where I had more tests. The consultant there left me in his consulting room and took off with my notes, along with his house doctor; they were gone for ages and I started to panic. The door then opened and they entered, both sitting on the edge of the table in front of me, swinging their legs. They looked at me in silence.

I thought: *Oh, Lord, this is it!*

Together, like Tweedledum and Tweedledee, they said: "We don't think you have lupus. We don't think you have ever had lupus."

Silence.

"Well, what on Earth was it?" I said. "First the scare of meningitis, then leukaemia... It must have been something more than sunstroke."

"It could have been a dose of sunstroke, which bordered on the danger mark, giving great concern. We'll never know," said the consultant.

I returned home, and when Val came home from school I said: "Book flights - we're going off to the sun, somewhere." It was soon to be half-term and a last-minute booking found us on a flying pencil, from Cardiff to Paris. We had a great time and it gave us ideas of further travels abroad.

It was some time later that my brain clicked in and I realized why there was no trace of lupus or any of the other hideous diseases mentioned when on such high alert. I rang Steve Morgan and thanked him for his ministry to me in hospital.

"It worked, Steve: I'm healed; there's no trace of anything. God is good."

"I'm so glad, Robert," he said. "I can add you to a long list of people the Lord has healed. Thank you for telling me."

More healing was to come through the ministry of this devout priest. Further laying-on of hands, in later years, healed ulcers in my oesophagus, which could have turned cancerous. Even later, chronic hay-fever, which interfered with conducting services - especially funerals (those lilies!) - simply went away. Whilst in Penarth I had been diagnosed with coeliac disease, which means that I cannot eat wheat (how ironic that bread was a central part of my life as a priest!) - it's a life-threatening disease, for which there is no cure, and it has to be controlled by a gluten-free diet. It's genetic and, unfortunately, Becky, my daughter, has it also.

What's next? I thought at the time. *What's next?!*

Cwmaman, 1995

'See, I am making all things new.'
Revelations 21:5

"O Lord, help me - I may have taken on more than I can chew!

"Why am I destined always to restore churches? Wouldn't it be wonderful if you sent me to a parish that was already restored, where there was a proper Parish Office, where the liturgy was already sorted?

"But, not my will, but thine!"

I decided to pop into St. Joseph's and do Evening Prayer there, instead of St. Margaret's, as I knew my curate would not be joining me. I wandered around, wondering how on Earth we could restore this building on a shoestring; I counted fifteen buckets and bowls collecting water from the leaking roof! The walls were green in places, the blocked flooring in a terrible state, and I came across a broken Rosary. "Just like the building," I said to God.

I decided to repair the Rosary. I searched around and found some twisties, stripped off the paper and used the wire to repair the Rosary - it didn't take long and soon the job was done. Then, I sat in the priest's stall, after removing fallen masonry, and offered the Sorrowful Mysteries for the restoration of the church - I chose the Sorrowful Mysteries because of the sorrowful state of the church. It was symbolic for me that the restored Rosary should be used to embrace the building with prayer, with a purpose of restoring the church.

We decided to set up a restoration appeal. We knew we couldn't do it with the professional builders that the Diocesan Advisory Committee required, so we invited them up to look at the state of the building.

"You must have Hook Mason to do the work," they told us. We also learnt that they wanted a million pounds to insure the site.

All of a sudden, one of our P.C.C. members slammed his walking stick on the floor, and said: "Listen here, you buggers-" I hid behind a pillar "-if you want this church restored, then you are going to have to let us do it with local builders and local resources."

There was deathly silence for a moment, then the archdeacon said that if we signed a document relieving the D.A.C. of any comeback, then they would allow it - we had to take full responsibility, if anything went wrong. We knew that the building couldn't be in any worse a state than it already was and that the least we could do was try, so we agreed and sent the D.A.C. packing.

Arrangements were made for a local builder to see to the roof, and a working party of parishioners from the existing parish of Aberaman and my new parish of Cwmaman did such a tremendous amount of work: walls were whitewashed, rubbish was thrown out in skips, the floor was sanded and the furniture polished, and put into some semblance of order, befitting a traditional church building. The end result was very pleasing, and minus the fifteen buckets.

This brought new life to the parish. The support of the parishioners was wonderful and, although it was still two separate parishes grouped together, there was hope of growth towards unity. It was hard work doing two of everything - two Holy Weeks, two Midnight Masses, two summer fetes, two Christmas bazaars... two of *everything* – but, with my loyal colleague, Father Bernard, I persevered because of their enthusiasm.

However, I knew that unless the building was regularly maintained, it could quite easily deteriorate again - something in the back of my mind told me that the Rosary hadn't quite finished its restorative, prayerful work.

It was years later, long after my day, that with generous grants the building had enjoyed a complete makeover, with a fitted kitchen, toilets, community area, modern sacristy, new organ and comfortable seating. Also, the powers that be finally decreed that the parish should be one united worshipping community.

The power of the Rosary never ceases to amaze me.

Cwmaman, 1996

'At this time the disciples came to Jesus and said "Who is the greatest in the kingdom of Heaven?" So, he called a little child to him whom he set among them. Then, he said "In truth I tell you, unless you change and become like little children, you will never enter the kingdom of Heaven. And so, the one who makes himself as little as this little child is the greatest in the Kingdom of Heaven."'
Matthew 18: 1-4

"There's been a terrible accident on the bypass," said Val: "a mother and child killed in a car crash."

"Oh, Lord, what a tragedy! Poor family - how awful for a family to lose two like that! I feel sorry for the priest who'll have to deal with all that," I said, as I was going through the door to church, for Mass.

When I came back from Mass, Val said that the undertaker had rung and could I ring him back. I did, and it transpired that *I* was the priest who would have to deal with all that - I was told to ring the mother/grandmother of the deceased, as the husband was in no fit state to deal with anything. I rang and made arrangements to visit.

I panicked a little, as I was still young to be dealing with such a tragic and unique situation as this. On my way to her house I prayed, as I always do in difficult circumstances: "O Lord, give me the words to say." I kept repeating this like a mantra, until I reached her house. I rang the doorbell and thought: *Here goes.*

Mrs. Bevan came to the door and, as she was letting me in, she said: "Oh, Vicar, I'm so sorry for you, having to deal with all this."

I was the one supposed to say that!!

What an incredible lady she was - we hit it off straight away. There was no bitterness, no anger towards God... all the things I was expecting. She even told me on one visit that she'd been to the hospital, to see the girl who had crashed into her daughter and granddaughter. She told the girl not to feel guilty, that she must live her life and put it all behind her. I couldn't believe such generous forgiveness and such wonderful Christian charity. This lady was a source of inspiration to me and has been ever since - I have told this story in homilies, throughout my ministry, to the astonishment of my congregations in all subsequent parishes.

She reminded me that Louise and Abigail had been to the nativity play in church, just weeks before. Abigail had stolen everyone's heart, dressed as an angel, talking to her mother, father, grandmother and myself in a loud voice, throughout the whole play. The family were worried that I would be cross, but I made it quite clear that she was not to be stopped - she was the star of the show!

Little did I know that I would be burying the little darling alongside her mother, very soon.

Mostly, when I visited Barbara, Louise's husband would be there. If not, I always made sure that I called to see him, which was very difficult, but he needed pastoral care - he was, after all, the next of kin.

The day of the funeral came and I braced myself; being an emotional person, I was terrified I would cry. However, nerves made that impossible - I was too preoccupied with the running order of the service to be emotional. Unbelievably, Barbara also helped, as you will learn soon. The church service was like nothing I had ever done before - there was an astonishing number of people in church and out on the street, because they couldn't get into St. Joseph's. We had children's hymns and children's readings from Sacred Scripture. All these years later, I can't remember what I said in my homily, but I know I took pains over it, for days and days before. It was a very solemn and moving service.

After the service the cortège left St. Joseph's Church and there were people lining the streets on the way out of the village. How moving that was! These were people who only knew the family by sight or by name, but Cwmaman, being the close-knit community it is, came together in support of this little family, in their darkest hour.

In the cemetery, at the graveside, it was devastating to see the two coffins, side by side - Louise's adult coffin and, of course, Abigail's tiny, white, child's coffin. Permission had to be granted for them to be buried in the same grave, as it is not lawful for this to happen; however, the tragic circumstances overruled the law, and I know it gave the family much comfort. It seemed appropriate, as Abigail was little more than a baby.

At the cemetery, we had to wait ages, for hordes of people to make their way to the graveside; needless to say, many people were quite some distance away. It seemed to me that practically everyone in church had come along.

As I was about to utter the words of the committal, Barbara came up to me and asked if I was alright. I nodded, and she held my hand throughout it all. Her faith was remarkable and carried her through this dark time in her life; I was, once again, so touched by her concern for me, at such a tragic moment in her life.

Most dedicated priests will tell you that priesthood is not a job but a vocation, and it is a huge privilege to minister to people during important times in their lives: times of joy, times of humour, times of celebration and times of sorrow. This situation brought all that home to me, in every sense of what we mean by "Sacred Priesthood".

In retirement I visited Barbara and was terribly saddened and shocked to hear that her husband had committed suicide, some time ago - he had never got over the loss of his daughter and granddaughter. Poor Barbara! All that she has had to go through, yet her faith still prevails.

May the souls of the faithful departed rest in peace.

Penarth, 1999

'Hear this, all you peoples, give heed, all who dwell in the world, men both high and low, rich and poor alike!'
Psalms 49:2

"How did the rehearsal go?" said Val.

"Fine," I said, "but I've just met a lady who looks like the queen and talks like the queen! I don't know what sort of a place we've come to!"

"They're no different to anyone else!"

"I know, I know - just a few jitters about taking on such a 'plum parish', as an old friend described it."

Like all parishes, the honeymoon period was great - I could do no wrong, almost walking on water. Then, once I tried to make some changes and implement what I had been trained and ordained to do, a few moans and groans could be heard... You get this everywhere - I have had it in all my parishes. One priest used to ask me: "How are the 'old guard' doing?"

Trying to bring the Gospel into situations like that can be very stressful, and it takes courage as a priest to persevere. It is only through the guidance of the Holy Spirit, along with the support of so many lovely parishioners, that I was able to do it. What is important to me is that the great majority of people in this wonderful parish responded with love, and we grew together, as priest and people; the "old guard" receded into the stonework and kept quiet.

It remains a very special place in my heart; we made so many lovely friends there. The standard of music was very high, from our wonderful organist, musical director and choirmaster Robert Court. The liturgy eventually became modern Catholic and, with the help of a number of wonderful curates, we achieved great things.

It was always a feeling of pride when Becky and Val would sing the *Responsorial Psalm*, or a solo part in the weekly anthem. Becky joined Robert's choir, "Cantemus Chamber Choir, Wales", and soon he was to ask Val to join as well. I know this gave them great pleasure, and still does today, even though Robert has retired.

The graveyard houses the grave of Joseph Parry, a famous Welsh composer - he composed the famous hymn tune *Aberystwyth and Myfanwy*. Many tourists would come to visit his grave and we had a centenary celebration concert for him while I was there - the American Joseph Parry Society organized it all; we welcomed many American visitors that day.

One lady said: "Gee, Father, I love that notice you have on the font."

I said: "Oh, thank you. It has met a need and actually works."

"Can I take a photo of it and send it to my priest at home, in the U.S.?"

"Of course."

We heard later that there is a church, somewhere in the U.S., with a replica of:

"The Church is a family,
and like all families
we welcome children.
When they make a noise
we are glad, because we
know they are here."

Tourists would come to visit St. Augustine's because it was a Butterfield church - a grade-A listed building and a landmark on the Penarth headland, which was seen for miles, even from the Severn Bridge. Keble College, Oxford, is also by Butterfield - that is where the very first Llandaff Diocesan Clergy School was held, in 1975. St. Augustine's Church featured on German maps during the second world war - it was used as a landmark by the Luftwaffe, making their way to bomb Cardiff docks. One historian told me of a war film, in which Hitler is pointing at a map, to my church, saying: "This is where you head for."

The church features in the poem *The Rime of the Ancient Mariner,* by Samuel Taylor Coleridge, in part one:

"The ship was cheered, the harbour cleared,
Merrily did we drop
Below the kirk, below the hill,
Below the lighthouse top."

...and also in part four:

"The harbour-bay was clear as glass,
So smoothly it was strewn!
And on the bay the moonlight lay,
And the shadow of the Moon.

"The rock shone bright, the kirk no less,
That stands above the rock:
The moonlight steeped in silentness
The steady weathercock."

We featured a tremendous number of wonderful concerts by Cantemus. One which always sticks in my mind is the two-hundredth anniversary of Trafalgar: they sang the Trafalgar Mass, and the procession of the choir at the start of the concert, with drum rolls, was awesome!

It was whilst in this parish that Archbishop Barry decided to make me a canon; as one lady said: "All of our rectors have been canons."

Good job he made me one, then! I wouldn't have wanted to let the side down.

The rectory was magnificent: a two-storey townhouse, near the town centre. The garden was a shambles, and I took it upon myself to work out my frustration at receiving so much criticism in the beginning, from a minority, to create a very splendid garden - it was deemed good enough to feature in the "Open Gardens Day" each year. It had a two-fold benefit: not only did I vent my frustrations, but we had many parish functions in the house and garden; all helped to build relationships which formed us into a loving, caring, worshipping community.

Whilst serving there, the archbishop asked me to incorporate the parish of Llandough into my existing parish. This was yet another challenge, but proved only to complement our expanding boundaries, with more faithful, loyal parishioners.

As with Aberaman, restoration was needed, and we were extremely lucky to have a tremendous amount of work done, costing well over half a million. St. Augustine's overlooked Cardiff Bay and the Millennium Centre - it was an incredible setting.

We were the first parish in Llandaff to introduce the "Christmas Tree Festival" - something which became very popular, and spread throughout the diocese and beyond. Nobody does it like Penarth, though: fifty or more decorated Christmas trees, all themed on the charity, business, school or organization they represented. It would be nothing to have two-thousand people walking through our church to look at the magnificent display of trees, whilst listening to various artistes perform: the Salvation Army, various choirs, and Becky, my daughter, to name but a few.

Penarth, 2005

'The Lord makes poor and makes rich; he brings low, he also exalts.' Samuel 2:7

"Guess what."

"What?" said Val.

"Barry has asked me to become a canon of the cathedral."

"Never!"

"Yes. I can't quite take it in."

Cuddles, kisses and phone calls to the family, who were over the moon! When Becky came home from school, she was ecstatic; Symon took it all in his stride.

The parish, too, was thrilled and actually paid for the cassock with crimson piping, the cape, the cincture, the cotta and the mozzetta. All of it was bought from a very expensive clerical outfitter; it cost an absolute fortune. Val and I went to Exeter for a fitting and stayed the night in a lovely hotel.

Thirty-one years after ordination, I found myself under that majestas again... for this ceremony. Once again awed; once again feeling unworthy.

It was a glorious day and it was very moving to see people from all my past parishes come to the cathedral. Afterwards, family, parishioners and friends came back to the rectory garden, for bubbly and a buffet.

I could only think of what my cousin Sue's husband, Peter,

had said when I was ordained: he said: "Rob, you've given your mother her dignity back, and her self-respect, after the way her marriage broke down. The indignity of returning to Neath in 1950, pregnant and husbandless, nearly destroyed her."

I felt: *If only she could see me now…!*

Well, of course she could! Looking down, proud as punch, telling all her cronies, gathered around a heavenly coffee-table: "He's a big-shot in that cathedral, now. Let's hope they don't fire this particular canon!"

One of my colleagues, Steven, congratulated me and said: "When we are dying of boredom in chapter meetings, I shall look over to you and, with a knowing smile, share the same thought: *'Goodness me, what we are we doing here? What has any of this got to do with the Gospel?'*"

I quickly realized that some of the canons had been chosen because of skills from previous professions: one had been a solicitor, one had been an accountant, another had been in the building construction industry, and another had been a managing director of a huge financial business. Were they going to expect me to inspect the steel inclusions here and there in the cathedral? Each was given a role to play and I cringed, but had the courage to say that I felt called on to be in a more spiritual role as a priest - something liturgical, pastoral; befitting the life of a priest. I had a few glares from one or two pharisaical members of the chapter, but I just sat in silence, as they made a note of my interest.

Penarth, 2005

'May he give you your heart's desire and fulfil every one of your plans.' Psalms 20:5

"Oh, look - there's an exhibition over there of Spanish homes," says Val; "let's have a look."

"We're certainly not buying anything," I said, in my *Scrooge* voice...

"Okay, Mister and Missus Donkin - just sign here and we'll sort out the rest. These flights are booked for you on 27th December, 2005, from Cardiff - only twenty-nine pounds each. Someone will greet you at the airport and take you to La Zenia four-star hotel. After you've settled in, one of our agents will pick you up and take you to various properties."

"Great," I said, rather nervously.

"We're not obligated to buy anything," says Val.

"I know, but it's a bit embarrassing, having had a cheap, four-day holiday in a four-star hotel... But, yes, you're right: we are not obligated," I said.

"You don't seem very interested in anything I've shown you," said the agent.

"Well, what we really want is a bit of 'real' Spain," said Val.

"I think I've got just the place," said the agent...

We came to a sleepy little Spanish village, called San Cayetano, and viewed the new development at the end of the village.

"Aren't the locals aggravated by this development?" I said.

"Well, all their husbands and sons are working on it, so I guess not," said the agent.

"Well, if you'd like to sign here," said our new Spanish solicitor, who could have been a boy in Val's class, "then the whole process will begin."

After an hour's drive to Alicante to sign, a trip to Orihuela to get Non-Residents Certificates, and a trip to a bank to set up an account, we nervously, but excitedly, started our Spanish journey!

It has to be the best adventure we have ever embarked upon together, as husband and wife. It took nearly two years before the property was ready and we finally signed the contract. It was fun to furnish and set up a home we could properly live in, for the first time in our married life - although we had a house in Wales which was rented out - because, of course, we were at the mercy of the Church in Wales, as to where we were forced to live. At first, of course, it was a holiday home, but since retirement, in September 2014, it has been our second home.

In those days, we had no idea there was an Anglican presence in the area. I knew about the diocese in Europe, certainly, but as holidaymakers, we were happy to attend the Spanish church in our village, on the Sundays within our holidays. Then, one day we met some people, who said they went to an Anglican service nearby - it was in a place called Los Balcones, and we decided to go one Sunday.

The church looked very unlike a traditional place of worship to me, and one lady explained that it had been built as a sports-centre, but the money had run out. However, it is only a building, and what is inside matters most. From that point of view, we had a wonderful welcome and I explained to the churchwarden that I would soon be retiring, and if I could be of any help, to just let me know.

When retirement came, and all the necessary permissions were received, I found myself on a rota, helping out in seven places of worship, within the chaplaincy of Ss. Peter and Paul, Torrevieja. One place of worship is only a room, dedicated to St. Teresa - it is situated in an exclusive golf resort; the other five are delightful churches, and space is rented by our Roman Catholic brothers and sisters, to celebrate Mass. Lago Jardin is an exception - it is a delightful little church, of which the chaplaincy has custody.

At that time there was an interregnum, and I was called upon every Sunday, when we were in Spain, even taking funerals and wedding blessings.

It has been a wonderful experience and has given purpose to my retirement. We were told that a new chaplain would be starting his ministry in November 2015, and we were all looking forward to that very much.

But, it has to be said, please or offend, that it was a shock to the system. Although the Church in Wales is a little bit old-fashioned in its liturgy (nevertheless, kosher), to find myself celebrating "Holy Communion", as they called it, and have mixed-up choices not even found in Common Worship, was a totally new experience for me, after forty years of priesthood. Holy Communion is the part of the Mass where the faithful approach the altar to receive the Precious Body and Blood of Christ. I can hear myself saying to myself: "What have I come to?"

All would be later restored to normality, and the beauty of liturgy enhanced, with the arrival of our wonderful new chaplain, Father Richard.

Penarth, 2007

'I am the resurrection and the life, he who believes in me shall never die.'
John 11:25

Rectory doorbell rings.

"Who's this, now?"

After a horrendously busy day, with two funerals, I just wanted to attend Evening Prayer with my curate, then get back home and have dinner with the family, followed by a large gin... or two. I opened the front door.

"Nick. Goodness me, what are you doing here?"

"I was in the area and decided to do the rounds and visit all the old gang. I've been to see Edward and he gave me directions to you; I rang John but couldn't get hold of him - I'll try again before I return home."

"Where are you staying?"

"I'm staying in the Marriott Hotel, in Cardiff. I've been here a few days but will return tomorrow."

"Well, if you'd said you were coming you could have stayed with us - Val would have loved to meet you. She's in work and won't be home until about six p.m; the kids are in school. What a shame."

"No, don't worry. I just wanted to revisit old haunts and see as many of the old gang as possible."

It was lovely to see him again. He seemed a little demure - not the old Nick I used to scold for his outrageous behaviour!

Later, I found that he had visited Edward, Christopher, David, Keith, Elfed, and Father David Thomas - chaplain at St. Michael's - and was now the bishop, with care for those who couldn't cope with the ordination of women: P.A.B. He also visited parishioners in Canton, where he played the organ on the Sundays, when he could. I felt that he was on a mission.

Then, some weeks later I read this, care of the *Bury Times*:

"The body of a missing priest, who regularly attended a Bury church, has been recovered from an estuary in Lancashire. Father Nicholas Clapp, who was due to conduct a service at Holy Trinity C.E. Church in Spring Street, on Sunday, vanished from his home in Preston, on Thursday, October 11th, leaving his dog behind.

"Divers were called to Preston dock on Tuesday morning, following reports of a body in the water. Police later confirmed the body was that of the 59-year-old missing priest.

"The Bishop of Blackburn - the Rt. Rev. Nicholas Reade - paid tribute to the semi-retired priest. He said: 'This is a tragic situation - the death of Father Nicholas will be mourned both by those in Lancashire and within the wider Church of England. Our thoughts and prayers are with all those who knew him, at this sad and difficult time.

"'Father Nicholas was known as a faithful priest in the Blackburn diocese, since retiring from parish ministry in 1998, because of the Church of England's decision to ordain women to the priesthood. His ministry to various parishes was widely appreciated.'

"Police say there are no suspicious circumstances surrounding the tragedy."

I wonder...

Earlier in life, while at St. Michael's, all of us students had to take part in a Parish Mission - the parish chosen was Father Peter Cobb's parish of Pencoed.

We were all allocated digs and I found myself with Nick, staying with Olga and Bryn. They were a lovely couple and gave us a wonderful welcome - we were made to feel really at home. I think Olga thought she was catering for two prospective bishops, with the amount of food and the quality of the cuisine, as well as the fuss she made of us.

You could never take Nick seriously, but couldn't help loving his wicked sense of humour.

One morning, over a sumptuous full-English breakfast, Olga came to our table in the conservatory with toast, to round the meal off. She exclaimed: "Oh, the tits are out!"

Nick and I looked at each other and desperately tried to stifle bursts of laughter. She was, of course, referring to the blue-tits in her beautiful garden.

Her high-pitched voice exclaiming this observation became a well-used slogan for us in the future, for the rest of our time in Llandaff: "The tits are out!" ...exclaimed in a high-pitched voice.

Later, I was to hear that Christopher had died.

What a wonderful friend and priest. We'd had such fun in Ystrad Meurig - bonds were formed there which were solid. He was so down to Earth - no airs and graces. He never assumed to be an intellectual, and had humble beginnings, in St. German's Church, in Cardiff, but the wonderful grounding in that Anglo-Catholic parish formed an incredible priest, with tremendous pastoral skills. Who needs a degree?

His parish of Llandaff North was packed to standing-room only on Sundays - he was loved by parishioners and the secular community alike.

I attended his funeral, but could only stand outside and listen to the funeral Mass through speakers, because the church was so cram-packed!

Later, I was to hear that Stuart had died.

Who's next?! I thought.

My memories of his insistent teaching that we must be "Born Again" resulted in a life-changing experience for me, which I have mentioned earlier. He was a wonderful friend.

*

Elfed died, also!

We were never really close, but he was still part of the gang.

Although he had divorced his wife and had a period of suspension from the Church in Wales, he returned as a chaplain to a nursing home, in my parish of Penarth.

May the souls of the faithful departed rest in peace.

Penarth, 2007

'For what does it profit a man to gain the whole world and forfeit his soul?'
Mark 8:36

Val came home from school and asked: "How did the funeral go?"

I said it was very sad - very moving. Then, I said: "Guess who made me a cup of tea."

Silence.

"None other than Sir Bryn Terfel."

I had been asked to conduct the funeral of the mother of a dear friend. Her mother had been a prominent parishioner in Pontrhydyfen - one of my former parishes. Meeting at the house for prayers, prior to the funeral, I arrived in good time, as always. With plenty of time to spare, I was offered a cuppa by this now-world-famous singer.

Not wishing to show off, he is now added to a little list of famous people I have met - these include: Richard Burton, Prince Charles, Princess Diana, Prince William, Prince Harry, Kelly Jones of *Stereophonics*, Rebecca Evans, the opera star, Denis O'Neil, the opera star, Lord Aberdare, Lady Treharne, Baroness Grey-Thompson (Tanni), and one famous artist, who is now infamous and in prison!

At Cwmaman I used to take Holy Communion to Kelly

Jones's grandmother. We were planning some fundraisers for St. Joseph's Church, and she sent me down to his house in Belmont Terrace, and told me to say that she had sent me to discuss possible events he could attend. I did go, but he was out, however I met him at a later time, in St. Joseph's, at a funeral - not the time or place to discuss fundraising.

Prince Charles visited the humble village of Tonmawr, at the opening of a new community centre. Princess Diana, Prince William and Prince Harry were present at a commemorative service in Llandaff cathedral, and as she was using the St. David's chapel to sign the register and various documents, we inevitably met her, as that was the chapel we always robed in; it was a very brief encounter and the princes were very young.

Rebecca Evans is an old friend from Pontrhydyfen, mentioned affectionately, elsewhere in this book; Denis O'Neil sang in St, Augustine's, Penarth, for a very special concert; Lord Aberdare had to listen to a sermon of mine, at St. Margaret's church, Mountain Ash – as mentioned earlier - and Lady Treharne had to endure a sermon in St. George's Church, in the village of St. George, in the Vale of Glamorgan. I was sent there as a student from St. Michael's, with the warden sitting at the back of the church, to assess me. Tanni was godmother, at a baptism in St. Augustine's.

After the assessment of my very first sermon, in placement, in the church of St. George, with Lady Treharne sitting beneath me, I tentatively waited for the report and assessment of my sermon. It came a few days later.

After Mass in the college chapel, making my way to the

refectory for breakfast, I looked in my pigeon-hole, and there it was - Og's handwriting could not be mistaken. I stuffed it in my pocket and proceeded to a sumptuous breakfast, served to perfection by our kitchen staff - headed by Maureen, whom we all adored.

After breakfast I rushed to my room, before making my way, with the others, to the University Faculty of Theology, to read this report.

It was good: Og reported that theological content was excellent and delivery was good. However, there was a comment: "Robert has the tendency to drop his gs, at the end of such words as 'working', 'hoping', 'loving', etc. This is quite common among people who come from the Neath/Swansea area of South Wales."

Og's final comment was: "Shockin'!"

Nick thought it was hilarious and so did the others. I was teased relentlessly at meal times and on other occasions - Nick would often say to me: "Are you *comin'* tomorrow, sunshine?" To which I would say: "P- off!"

Penarth, 2008

'I am the Lord, I have called you in righteousness, I have taken you by the hand and kept you; I have given you as a covenant to the people.' Isaiah 42:6

"How long have you been here now, Rob?" said Bishop David - the assistant bishop and a dear friend.

"Just coming up to ten years," I said.

"Do you think you'll stay here until you retire?"

"I suppose so, at least. If I'm going to move it needs to be now, really, to give a fair amount of time to a new parish, because retirement isn't that far away."

We were in his car, going to the churchwarden's house for a parish review. He had popped in to say hello to Val, then we made our way, having this conversation en route. My words - "If I'm going to move it needs to be now" - will remain in my ears for a long time to come.

The review with all the wardens, treasurer and curates went well, we had refreshments and made our way home. Bishop David dropped me off at the rectory and I poured a gin and tonic. I felt relieved it was over and we'd ticked every box - even though David was a friend, he still represented the hierarchy.

The next morning, the phone goes…

"Robert, it's Barry here," as if I didn't recognize the

archbishop's voice. "I wondered if you would consider going to the parish of Caerphilly."

Deathly silence!

"Oh, I'm sorry if I've said something out of turn. It was just something that Bishop David said this morning in our staff meeting."

I'll kill him, I thought. "No, it's alright; I just hadn't thought about it, really. I'll have to discuss it with Val, and the thing is that we're off to Spain tomorrow, for the half-term holiday."

"You go off to Spain and have a lovely time, then let me know what you've decided when you come home."

"Okay."

"It's just that nobody has applied for the parish, and it's one of the key parishes in the diocese, as you know. Actually, I should say that one person *did* apply for it, but he was an inexperienced curate from England, and would have been totally unsuitable for such a large, demanding parish."

We concluded our conversation with niceties and I put the receiver down, rather stunned.

When Val came home from school she commented that it was going to be a wonderful half-term holiday in Spain, and talked about changing our lives, yet again: another move and another parish, which was probably another big challenge!

We went to our apartment in Spain and discussed the ins and outs. We realized that Rebecca would be concerned, as she still lived with us and was a stone's throw away from her place of work, at W.N.O.

We decided to go. We returned home from Spain and told

Barry.

Rebecca declared that she wouldn't be coming to live in Caerphilly, so we immediately set out for Cardiff Bay and drove around, looking for any properties for sale which might be suitable for her. The Lord was on our side, as we found a perfect one-bedroom apartment in a gated community, just a walk from the Millennium Centre, where W.N.O. was housed.

But our looking for houses didn't end there.

The archbishop had told me that there was going to be a new house built in the grounds of the old rectory, and it would probably be ready by the time we moved.

Laugh out loud! It hadn't even been started!

Due to difficulties with Caerphilly Borough Council, nobody could even really say *when* it would be built.

Too late now: we'd agreed to go!

The archdeacon - another personal friend - told me they were looking for a temporary house to put us in, while the new rectory was being built. Everything the local estate agent came up with seemed reasonably fine with us, as a temporary home, but the maintenance manager of the parsonage board always turned them down: it had to have four bedrooms; it had to have a suitable room to be used as a study… we lost count of the number of houses we were asked to look at. In the end, the archdeacon suggested that in our spare time we look around by ourselves, which we did.

The estate agent was a childhood friend of Val's and that helped greatly. His parents had a chalet in Freshwater, Pembroke, and he and his brother used to play with Val and her sisters, all those years ago. It was the place where we spent the second half of our honeymoon.

He rang one day: "Val, Charles here. Do you like the colour blue?"

"Well, yes I do, actually. Why?"

"I've found a house that might suit, at last. However, it's decorated in blue throughout."

"Okay, we'll look at it - just give us the address."

We loved it. It had four bedrooms, three bathrooms, a suitable separate room for a study, kitchen-diner, a wonderful back garden and, yes, it was blue! Even the front-door key was blue!

"Kerry isn't going to like this, so don't get too excited," said Val.

"He's on holiday. Let's just tell Chris and David and hope for the best."

Chris, the archdeacon, thought it was great, as long as we were happy, whilst David, the assistant bishop - whose fault all this was, anyway – didn't even visit, just looked at it on the internet and gave his approval. The deal was done before Kerry, the maintenance manager, came home.

It was prudent that so much time was taken finding a suitable house, because it wasn't six months, but three years that we lived there, due to Caerphilly Borough Council's inefficiency, unscrupulous methods and, I believe, downright anti-Church attitudes. The only support we had was from the town mayor, who happened to be the brother of Charles, the estate agent, and another Freshwater childhood friend of Val's.

We loved living there and tried to persuade the powers that be that with a few alterations and extensions it could easily have made a very suitable rectory, but Kerry was having none of it!

Caerphilly, 2011

'But he said, "Blessed rather are those who hear the word of God and obey it!"'
Luke 11:28

"Here we go," I said; "this is the eighth move we've made, and for such a short time. If only they'd listened to us: the 'blue house' could have made a wonderful rectory."

However, we did enjoy creating a new home (yet again), and the expense was covered by my dear mother-in-law, together with the laughable diocesan "disturbance allowance" which wouldn't even cover one room in *any* house. The new rectory was a purpose-built house, which took three years. It was lovely to have a proper study/office, separate to the rest of the house, so that the family would not have to encounter anyone coming to see me pastorally.

We opened the house and garden, as we always did in every home, for certain events, and this helped deepen our relationship with many lovely parishioners. It was sad to me that we were not able to do this three years previously, when we first arrived - it has always been a wonderful p.r. tool and Val has always supported me, when not many wives would tolerate it. I am so grateful for her team spirit, in welcoming the parish into our homes. As I said, it was a pity we couldn't do it the moment we arrived in the parish, in 2008.

When I was visiting the parish with the archdeacon and churchwardens - looking at the three churches, discussing the housing problem and, most importantly, the liturgy - Chris looked at me, after visiting the third church, and said: "Is it the liturgy that's the problem, Robert?"

I must have had a face like my mother's - she could never conceal her inner feelings and I've inherited that gene.

Genes, again...

"Well, the thing is, I've not used the *Green Book* since 1995, and I've never in my life taken matins as the main service on a Sunday morning."

The *Green Book* was a disaster for the Church in Wales. In the 1960s, work was done by the Liturgical Commission, which produced a little blue book: an experimental modern rite of the Mass - it was soon hailed as avant-garde by other provinces of the Anglican Communion, and even commented on by Rome. Unfortunately, the experiment went on for nearly twenty years, and in that time the Church of England had moved from a similar revision, called *The Alternative Services Book to Common Worship*, whilst Rome, with Vatican II, had produced their modern Mass. In 1984, the Church in Wales came up with an old-fashioned, uninspiring, stilted prayer book, which lacked everything other denominations were already enjoying. Protests soon resulted in a modern alternative rite, which became definitive in 2004.

"Well, I'm sure we could manage to introduce the service, if that's important to you," said one of the churchwardens. I gave it some thought and, with that agreement, decided to go to the parish.

On my first Sunday I found that there was a produced leaflet, with some of the modern rite included - a mix-match of various liturgies. I explained that this was no good and that we should be using the full rite.

Someone, without my knowledge, went to the Church in Wales's head office, in Cathedral Road, Cardiff, and came home with three-hundred copies of my new rite. If I had been given a say, I could have saved a fortune, by creating a professionally-produced, user-friendly booklet; and, I would not have introduced this before a vital explanation of the above history, careful preparation, teaching and instruction, over a period of time, maybe using Easter Day as a launch date. Alas, on day one some were up in arms, some stopped coming and insulting emails and letters were received. I was old and ugly enough to ignore them, and too long in the tooth not to treat them with the contempt they deserved; however, it was hard work from that moment on to get people to trust me.

Glad to say that (apart from the customary old-guard), with the help of supportive curates, a wonderful treasurer and a rector's warden, and with much needed constitutional corrective measures, regarding the structure of P.C.C. and sub-churchwardens, the parish started to grow.

In the end, we were sad to leave a wonderful group of people in each church, who had vision and determination in the mission of the Church. My retirement do was held in St. Martin's and Archbishop Barry graciously came to preach - it was very moving. The parish went to town with the hog roast and other refreshments, whilst Val and I provided the wine. By then we had already left the parish and moved into our own house... at last! We flew to Spain, using holiday time due to me, and had a couple of weeks there, before coming back for the actual last Sunday and farewell service.

I had always wanted to serve in a church dedicated to my personal patron saint - born on St. Martin's day, this was something I truly wanted; the Lord heard my plea!

Still, a priest never retires – I have found that out in our beloved Espana.

Caerphilly, 2012

'Let your fountain be blessed, and rejoice in the wife of your youth.' Proverbs 5:18

Phone goes...

"Father Robert speaking."

"Oh, hello - this is the B.B.C. here. We have a young couple who want to get married in your church and want to feature them in our series *Don't Tell The Bride*."

"Oh, really? I'll have to check with the church authorities to see if this is allowed."

"We've spoken to the archdeacon and he says that it's up to you."

In spite of this I rang the bishop's office and was told to go for it, as it would put Caerphilly on the map and be a good promotion for the church. No pressure then.

I met with the producers of the show first and explained that it was important for me, as a priest, that they be properly interviewed and prepared. They agreed, their only stipulation being that the bride couldn't be there, as the whole point of the show is that she only knows they are getting married, but has no idea where.

Hmmm...

We overcame the problem by having her sister present, who would convey the matrimonial teaching to the bride after the big day, using an instruction booklet that I use as part of wedding preparation; I wasn't entirely happy, but went along with it in the end.

John was a nice young man, and I learned that his father's funeral had been conducted by my predecessor at St. Martin's; although he had never darkened its doors since, the church was very special to him. How many times have I heard that, and similar stories?

The initial interview and successive preparation session were filmed, as was the rehearsal the night before. Florists took over, doing all the silly things that I wouldn't normally allow, and the church looked like a flower festival; I had a feeling that the producers wanted to "brighten up" what they saw as a "dull" venue, to create a spectacular wedding. I was already beginning to regret the whole thing and couldn't wait for the following day to come and go.

It came...

The service was conducted as a proper service of Holy Matrimony should be, and everyone was very pleased with the way everything turned out. The bridal party left for Caerphilly castle, for the reception, and I returned home, relieved. However, when the programme was shown on *BBC Three* we sat to watch it and we were taken aback at the bride's attitude. She kept saying to her father: "I wonder where the wedding is going to take place?" I tried to see the funny side of it but was appalled when, as she entered St. Martin's Road, she was heard to say: "Oh, no - it's going to be that stupid church, isn't it?"

Val's comment was that they should change the title of the

programme to *Don't Invite The Bride*.

We laughed and I vowed: *Never again… never, ever again!*

Spain, 2015

'Therefore, my beloved, be steadfast, immovable, always excelling in the work of the Lord, because you know that in the Lord your labour is not in vain.'
Corinthians 15:58

At last, we have a chaplain, I thought. *Perhaps I won't be so busy now!*

Laugh... out... very... loud... indeed!!

The Venerable Richard Seabrook was licensed on 15 November in Los Balcones Church, Torrevieja.

The bishop wasn't there but the Archdeacon conducted the ceremony which was very inspirational. I felt privileged to be part of it all and couldn't wait to meet this priest properly. Since then we have become such good friends and I just love being in Spain, helping him out whenever possible.

After serving in parishes in England he then served in Australia for eleven years before coming to Spain. He and I have the same love of the Mass, of liturgy in general, of how things should be conducted. We are Catholic in our priestly life and share the same feelings about the life of the Church.

I like to think that Father Richard has become a personal friend and he often spends time with us in Spain and Val and Becky adore him.

He has given new life to my ministry in retirement. I cringe when I think of some clergy I know who retire and ditch ministry as if they had just left a tiresome job in a supermarket! I even know one who has got another part time job in a pub, never wears clerical clothes, rarely attends church on Sundays! Was it a vocation or what? Was it a calling or just a job that provided a house and a bit of status in the community?!

I could think of more profitable ventures!

I don't think I am unique, in fact I know I'm not! I always say that I was called in the womb. Consecrated there, if you like.

With some of these memoirs I am recalling, how on earth could I just walk away, live as a recluse, abandon church and live like a lay person or even as a secular person? No, one is a priest until one dies.

At home in Wales I have a PTO and help out when needed. It must be a source of frustration to some of my colleagues that when they want help I appear to be in Spain.

All this makes for a fulfilled life in retirement and I can honestly say that I am thoroughly enjoying it.

No PCC Meetings, no church committees, no Easter Vestry Meetings; no silly people unwilling to call me Father, no people living in the past wanting old forms of liturgy unwilling to see that liturgy is like a special communication with the Lord and needs to be continually revised.

Just look at how communications have changed over the last 50 years!

From one phone in the hallway to the current mobile phone that does everything, to say nothing about the internet and emails.

I can remember a very arrogant teacher in one parish complaining about changes I had made! I said that as a teacher she no doubt used all modern forms of technology with her students, or did she still use a blackboard and paper and pencil?!

She peevishly admitted that it was the former style of modern instruction used in her classroom. Also when it comes to clothes I pointed out that like myself, she probably delighted in having new clothes from time to time! Or did she wear the same old coat from years and years ago!

I made my point and while I was at it I said that as far as incense was concerned, what person didn't like a beautiful perfume!

Back to the point, also in retirement there are no Clergy Schools to attend, no buildings to maintain, no church finances to worry about, no Returns to the Archdeacon, No Archdeacon breathing down my neck!

I have to be careful as my present boss in Spain is an Archdeacon! However, a mark of his humility is that he doesn't want to use his title and simply wants to be a priest and goes by Father. Father Richard.

Ministry there is so different. One time when Father Richard was on holidays the phone went…

"Hello, Father Robert, can you do a funeral for us please?"

"When?"

"Tomorrow!"

"Tomorrow! Well, yes I can but you'll have to explain to the family that I will not have time now to visit them. I'll have to arrive early to the Crematorium and discuss things with them there!"

"That's no problem, I'll inform the family."

"Can you give me a phone number so I can at least speak to the widow today?"

That is a typical scenario with regard to funerals in Spain.

The distance between each church is quite something, so different from a parish in the UK where all the churches are in the same town or neighbourhood. Father Richard told me once that this was nothing to him as the distance between churches in Australia meant that sometimes he would have to stay overnight.

It is wonderful, in retirement, to be free of the ties and restrictions of being 'in office.' I don't miss the challenges of having to change things for the better in parishes and having to introduce new things!

Father Richard has done a wonderful job doing this in the Chaplaincy and has shown such patience in a professional, dignified and priestly way, far better than I ever did! I think we can all be grateful for his superb ministry. It makes me proud that we are Anglicans which means we are Catholic and Reformed.

Heol-Y-Gelli, 2016

'Grandchildren are the crown of the aged, and the glory of children is their parents.'
Proverbs 17:6

"Mam, Dad, we've got something to tell you," said Symon.

My heart sank for a moment, thinking something was wrong.

"Cath is pregnant!"

"Oh, that's fantastic! When? When?" says Val.

"It's due around the end of April," says Cath.

Emelia-Rose was born on 24th April 2016 - the most delightful, beautiful, stunning, gorgeous baby girl (not biased!!!) - Val and I were thrilled. We didn't think we would ever be grandparents and Emelia is such a wonderful, placid, easy to care for child, that she is a joy to have around - we love to have her visit, and we fall into the role of Granny and Grandad with great joy.

She has given us so much pleasure, because she has brought us together as a family, much more closely. Auntie Becky is besotted, and she and Symon are now closer than ever, as brother and sister. Cath has just slipped into our family, as if she's always been there, and she is the most delightful partner for Symon; I think she deserves a medal for putting up with him!

Like all youngsters in this modern age, everything is done backwards: move in together first, baby next, then comes the baptism, and next, the wedding! Why have things reversed? In our day it was the wedding first, then move in together, then the baby, and the whole joyful experience culminated with the baptism - one tier of the wedding cake was used as a baptismal cake! Can you beat that? Absolutely not.

However, the most important thing is that their love for each other, and for Emelia-Rose, is sound, and will grow - my prayers will continue for this to be the case.

I am so proud that Symon has risen to the challenge of being a dad - I still think of him as my little boy! To think that he is now a father makes me really feel my age. Such feelings always take me back to my childhood and lack of a father - I know that, until I get to my grave, I will always feel deprived of a father's love. I have this fantasy that we will meet in the next life, and that all will be well. My prayers for the departed members of my family always include him, my mother, Val's departed loved ones, and also Elsie, in fact. I hope that those prayers will secure him a place in the Kingdom of Heaven.

It always fascinated me that Symon should be a carpenter and joiner, following in the footsteps of his paternal grandfather. Genes are powerful things! I can see traits of my mother, my mother-in-law, father-in-law, Val and myself in both Symon and Rebecca, but I often wonder what traits they and myself have inherited from Georgie-Porgie-Pudding-and-Pie. Could it be my coeliac disease, my mood swings, my flying off the handle, my stress over things, my anger at stupid, greedy, money-grabbing politicians... who knows?! All I know is that the Lord has walked with me, talked with me and carried me from the womb to my present life, and I have always said that I am yet to know his real purpose for me, in my priestly life. At the time of writing I am sixty-seven, and am waiting with bated breath to see what he will yet do with me.

I am at your service, Lord - do with me as you will!

Or, as the psalm says: "Here I am, Lord - I come to do your will."

San Cayetano, Spain, 2018

'For you have rescued my soul from death, you kept my feet from stumbling that I may walk in the presence of God and enjoy the light of the living.'
Psalms 56:14

And, what was His will for me next?

Well, it was a heart attack!

"You're looking well, Father Robert," said one of the congregation, at Los Balcones.

"Yes, I'm fine, thank you. It's been quite busy since Father Richard has been away, but you know how much I love helping out. The next time he goes on holidays, I'm making him take me with him!" Laugh out loud!

"Yes, we're so lucky to have you; it's very much appreciated."

"I know it is, but it's my pleasure. He's home tomorrow and I've got a funeral in the morning, then it's over to him."

The funeral went well and I returned home to make some lunch.

After a siesta, I did some shopping; just enough for one, to last until Saturday, when I was due to fly home - Val had already gone home for a rehearsal and concert. I did some reading, checked with the San Cayetano Friends that we were still meeting for coffee in the morning, and checked that Father Richard was still able to go out for a meal to catch up, before I returned home. Wednesday was the day and it was to be at La Tropical; we had tried to have a meal there once before, but he was too unwell. I then made my evening meal and watched some television.

At about 10.30 p.m., I suddenly felt exhausted and decided to go to bed. Climbing the stairs, I felt short of breath and put it down to a chest infection; Val and I had thought about this on the Saturday before - the day she travelled home: I had complained of wheeziness and a pain in my left arm, and we thought it might be something I had picked up.

In the middle of the night, nature called and, on getting to the bathroom, I found myself gasping for breath. I went downstairs and made a cup of tea, but could hardly climb back upstairs without gasping.

Definitely a chest infection, I thought; *must go to the health centre in the morning.*

I got up early, made my way to the health centre and Antonio, the receptionist, gave me an appointment for 10.50 a.m. I returned at said time and waited to be called.

Between my pigeon-Spanish and the doctor's pigeon-English we realized there was a problem with my pulse. He called the nurse in - who had good English - and she brought a more sophisticated machine to take my pulse, as the doctor had failed to.

She then flew back into her room, came back with a tablet and told me to put it under my tongue, then get to the hospital as soon as possible, but not to drive.

I went over to the bar where the San Cayetano Friends had arranged to meet, and told them I had to go to the hospital. They were aghast and told me that I was grey! Glyn said: "You're not driving - I'm taking you!"

We are so lucky to have a university hospital just five minutes away from our village in Spain. I gave the letter the doctor in the health centre had given me to the receptionist, and she gave me a card with a number on it; I sat and kept my eye on the screen for my number - I didn't have to wait long before it came up.

In an observation room, the doctor looked at the letter and I had an E.C.G. Within ten minutes I was in "Urgencias" (accident and emergency). There, I was given another E.C.G., blood-pressure check, put on a drip and given oxygen. At this point I still thought it was a chest infection.

Sue and Glyn came over later with some essentials - so kind; so thoughtful. The nurses wouldn't let Glyn in, which alarmed me a little bit: only one visitor at a time. *Why?* I wondered.

Later on, I complained that I was still out of breath - the tube feeding me oxygen didn't seem to be doing anything. The doctor said something to a nurse and within two minutes I'd had another E.C.G.

When she tore off the print-out and gave it to the doctor, he shouted: "Madre mia!" Within minutes I was in U.C.I. (intensive care). There, I had another E.C.G., an x-ray, a more sophisticated oxygen mask, back on the drip, another blood-pressure check, doctors and nurses fussing around me... I thought I'd had it - I thought the Lord was going to take me!

The care was astonishing. I realized there was a problem, but couldn't find the right Spanish to ask: chest... pneumonia?

Val quickly found a flight and returned on Thursday. This was the day I was having a procedure, in Cartagena hospital.

I still wasn't very clear about things, but when I got there the doctor spoke perfect English; he told me I'd had a heart attack and that he was going to put three stents in and repair an artery. It was quite amazing, and a little bit scary, to be lying on a slab, watching the whole thing on a screen, the doctor giving me a running commentary as he proceeded.

It took a while but, thankfully, he was successful. I thanked him, but he waved it off, as if to say it was all in a day's work.

I was duly returned to Los Arcos Hospital, by which time Val had arrived with Sue and Glyn. Between Sue, Glyn, Rod and Mary, Val was well looked after; I know that Margaret and Lindsay would have been helping hands as well, but they were in Turkey, visiting their son and grandchildren. Sue was in England, having a hip operation, so Steve was preoccupied with that. However, all our friends, including Marion and Joe, kept in touch, thanks to *WhatsApp*. As for me, I felt safe in the hands of these wonderful doctors and nurses! I could only thank God for such amazing medical care.

One nurse asked me what sounded like: "Quieres pepi?" I knew that "quieres" means "do you want", but "pepi" was a new one on me. In the end, she asked the young doctor what it was in English and he, quite nonchalantly, with a deadpan face (not realizing it was a slightly inappropriate word), simply said: "Piss." She turned to me and said: "Quieres piss?"

Father Richard came to visit seven times in all. He came three times to the hospital, to bring me the sacrament, and three times to our apartment. The first time he came was the day after it all happened.

I said: "We were supposed to be in La Tropical tonight."

"We'll make it one day," he said.

I wondered if I should ask him for the last rites; I was so frightened by then.

We finally managed to book a meal in La Tropical, as a thank-you to him for his wonderful pastoral care, before returning to Wales. I had a follow-up appointment with the cardiologist in Los Arcos, who spoke good English and explained everything. I returned to our apartment, with prescriptions for no less than ten tablets.

Whilst the medical side of things ran efficiently and smoothly, the prescription side of things was hilarious. The system in Spain is to purchase the medication, then, after the doctor has signed and stamped the prescriptions, get the money back. It took three trips to the health centre in the village, a visit to a health centre in Cartagena, a visit to the health centre in Torre Pacheco, three visits to Los Arcos hospital and four visits to the pharmacy, before they were finally stamped and signed properly - our fault, for not knowing the system. The pharmacist in the village was greatly amused in the end, because she kept pointing to the corner where we needed the stamp and signature; these prescriptions had more stamps and signatures than any other document in España! We were duly reimbursed for one-hundred and thirty euros.

After a fortnight in hospital and a fortnight in our apartment, we returned to Wales. I was so glad to see my family, whom I thought I would never see again.

The Lord still has a purpose for me and I will be guided by his hand. One is a priest until the end of one's days.

TODAY

Perhaps my whole life has been *astoundin'* (as Og would say), and I pray to God that it continues in his service for a lot longer. I love him so much - he has been the Father that my mother said would never let me down.

As I open my eyes every morning, holding the Blessed Rosary, this is my prayer:

"My day begins and ends with you, Lord God.

"In the meantime, walk with me, talk with me, guard me, guide me, keep me and my family safe from all the snares of the Evil One and all our enemies, and may your glorious reign of peace begin today.

"Maranatha! Come, Lord Jesus - come today."

Then follows the Divine Office and the powerful Prayer of the Rosary of the Blessed Virgin Mary. I could fill another book with petitions that have been answered via this most holy and sacred prayer.

'Praise the Lord Jerusalem, Zion praise your God.'
Psalms 147:12

A TIME TO WEEP AND A TIME TO LAUGH

REV. CANON ROBERT DONKIN

About the author

Robert was called to the Priesthood at 16 and was guided towards Ordination by local priests.

After school he worked in the Briton Ferry Steel Works in South Wales, part of the Dupont Group. He later studied at St. John's College, mid Wales and then St. Michael's College Llandaff, Cardiff.

Robert was ordained in 1974 at 23 years, the youngest a priest can be, according to Canon law. He has served in many parishes in South Wales, before becoming a Canon of Llandaff Cathedral in 2005 and serving on the Cathedral Chapter for 9 years. Robert has been ordained for 42 years and has been an honorary priest in the Chaplaincy in Spain since retirement in September 2014.

Robert enjoys cooking, reading, gardening, languages, all types of music and of course writing.

About the publisher

L.R. Price Publications is dedicated to publishing books by unknown authors.

We use a mixture of both traditional and modern publishing options to bring our authors' words to the wider world.

We print, publish, distribute and market books in a variety of formats including paper and hard back, e-books, digital audio books and online.

If you're an author interested in getting your book published; or a book retailer interested in selling our books, please contact us.

www.lrpricepublications.com

L.R. Price Publications Ltd,
27 Old Gloucester Street,
London, WC1N 3AX.

020 3051 9572

publishing@lrprice.com

REV. CANON ROBERT DONKIN

A TIME TO WEEP AND A TIME TO LAUGH

Printed in Great Britain
by Amazon

10148593R00129